To: ♡
From: Randy 2012

Once More With Feeling

Once More With Feeling

A Book of Classic Hymns & Carols

Selected by Rupert Christiansen

Woodcuts by Marianne Fox-Ockinga
Music transcribed by Anne-marie Bulpitt

SHORT BOOKS

First published in 2007 by
Short Books
3A Exmouth House, Pine Street
London EC1R OJH

10 9 8 7 6 5 4 3 2

A CIP catalogue record for this book is available from the British Library.

Jacket design: James Nunn

ISBN 978-1-906021-16-0

Printed in Great Britain by Clays Ltd, Suffolk

CONTENTS

Introduction *p.7*

A Brief History of the Hymn *p.15*

Hymns *p.23*

Carols *p.171*

Miscellany *p.218*

Bibliography *p.224*

Introduction

Even in an age as benighted as ours, its spiritual life flattened by prim multiculturalism, yar-boo-sucks atheism and mindless materialism, the great hymns and carols of the Protestant tradition retain their unique capacity to bring us together. It is to their fervent eloquence and broad melodies that we turn in times of trouble and celebration: not just weddings, funerals and Christmas, but any occasion which calls to be marked or memorialized with solemnity or dedication, be it the beginning of a term, the end of a war or the FA Cup final. The collective singing of hymns marks not just faith in the battered but resilient Christian gospel of love, but also an assertion that we are ultimately One, not just in God but in our humanity.

This selection is inevitably personal and partial, but I hope not wildly eccentric. I guess that my taste is typical enough: I'm middle-aged and come from the warm reasonable heart of middle England. Religion does not torment me. To the insistence of Richard Dawkins and his kind that God is a delusion, I would retort with William Cowper's sage warning that 'Blind unbelief is sure to err'. My family paid its respects to Anglicanism, and I still feel deep affection (albeit increasingly tinged with exasperation at the timidity and shilly-shallying of its Establishment) towards its cardinal virtue of accepting the moral and material realities of existence with tolerance rather than judgment.

And my vague but unbreakable affiliation to its simple creed has allowed me access to a treasure-trove of music and poetic language. Throughout the formative years of my childhood, I sang the hymns in this book until they became hard-wired. Filed in some recess of my brain, they remain ready to be downloaded as the case requires: struggling home past crowds, wind and rain I mutter 'Onward Christian Soldiers' through clenched teeth; drumming my fingers on the steering wheel in suppressed rage at a traffic jam gets me going on 'Guide me, O thou great Redeemer'; sitting in hospital corridors awaiting the good or bad news, it is 'Lord of all hopefulness' that buoys me up.

Yet it wasn't primarily through churchgoing that all this soaked in – even in the early 1960s, there was seldom enough congregation at St Olave's to get a good old blast going (after Matins, I vividly remember cycling home past the Baptist tabernacle and being amazed that you could hear its congregation singing from the street). No, I associate hymns far more with my prep school, where the music was in the capable hands of the headmaster's wife.

Mrs Lintott – I believe her Christian name was Edna, which might have explained why she kept it so very quiet – was a beaky-nosed, bossy old bag in brown brogues and a tweed skirt. But she was also a gifted pianist who could boogie-woogie with the best of them as well as knock off the Schubert Impromptus - both of which she did during her turn at the end-of-term concert. Her imaginatively programmed carol concert was a highlight of the calendar, and the school choir which she coached and conducted was considered crack. One year, we won some regional competition or other, I remember, with our rendition of John Blow's melancholy anthem 'O pray for the peace of Jerusalem'. In the coach on our triumphant way back from Lancing Chapel, we sang hymn after hymn, pausing only for a magical stop at a greasy spoon where we feasted on the rare and glamorous treat of egg and chips washed down with Coca-Cola.

I learnt the standard repertory at the Sunday morning service which took place before our weekly exeat in the school hall. Three congregational hymns and an anthem from the choir were interspersed with two lessons (one read by us, the other by a master) and a few prayers and responses – forty years on, this still ranks as my ideal form of worship, perhaps because it heralded some glorious hours of liberty. When we returned to jail in the evening, sated with roast beef and sweets and telly, there was another equally lovable but more intimate ritual – a sobering fifteen minutes of compline, in minor key and twilight mood, before cocoa and buns and the dorm. 'We will now sing Hymn 137, omitting verses 4 and 5' are words that bring me out in a Proustian rush of remembrance. Be assured, however, that verses will not be omitted in such cavalier fashion here.

We sang lustily, joyously even, in uninhibited treble

and alto, and there was no shame at being good at hymns – they were a pleasure, not a chore, as much fun as the Beatles and the Beach Boys. Membership of the choir was as respected a badge as membership of a First Eleven or being top in Maths, and even the skinny bespectacled nerd Lewis Forbes-Pritchard – he looked like Dan Dare's arch-enemy the Mekon – was envied for his ability to sing a soaring piercing descant in tune.

The rot set in when I went on to public school. Voices began to break, bringing anxiety about the sounds that would emerge from our hormonally assailed vocal cords, and cynicism set in as to conventional hymnly sentiments of greater love and light divine. Even 'Jerusalem' – than which there is no hymn more masculine and noble – couldn't get more than a turgid growl out of us. Our rendition once so enraged the headmaster at the beginning-of-term assembly that he stopped us after the first verse, commanded a replay and threatened us with iron rations and forced labour on the vegetable patch if it didn't shape up. 'Now, school,' he exhorted in conclusion, 'Once more with feeling. Or else.' The organ resumed. The bollocking made a little bit of difference, but not much, and half of us still came in before the springing offbeat which Parry so brilliantly insists on.

It was many years before I recovered my joy in singing hymns. The patina of adolescent cool wasn't the only factor contributing to this falling off – the hymns themselves sold out, as the end of the 1960s saw the inexorable rise of the modernisers. A great mistake in my view: sermons and psalms may have been part of the liturgical problem but not the hymns, and nobody knew how to sing the new ones – quite apart from the fact that their skiffle-band, youth-club jauntiness seemed as silly, patronising and hypocritical as the Latin teacher who affected beatnik blue jeans and a roll-neck jumper. 'God of Concrete, God of Steel'? 'Dance then wherever you may be,/ I am the Lord of the Dance said he'? Come on, guys, who're ya trying to kid? Any fool could tell that behind that fixed-grin New Seekers chumminess was something emotionally flaccid – either a wan folksiness or an insidious jauntiness, bloodless and phoney in comparison with the organ-powered ardour of 'Who Would True Valour See'. Why muddy the waters? Let the Grateful Dead and Frank Zappa do their funky transgressive thing, and let the hymns stay pure in their earnest moral uplift.

I say everybody found the modern hymns a turn-off, but of course, that's not true: lots of people, mostly of an evangelical persuasion, like these 'worship songs', and I guess they have established themselves, along with phenomena like coffee in the vestry and the kiss of peace that have alienated others, including myself, from the dear old Church of England. Ysenda Maxtone-Graham's marvellous study of Anglicanism's terminal dither, *The Church Hesitant*, points out that both sides in this stylistic debate abuse each other across a chasm of paper-tiger caricature – 'cathedral musicians go '"Jesus, Jesus, yeah, I love you, I want you", with imaginary guitars, and evangelicals mimic the worst Victorian hymns in vibrato.' It's true that the canon of classics constantly needs reassessing and refreshing, that Isaac Watts and Charles Wesley were considered shockingly innovative by the eighteenth-century establishment, and similar disdain met the 'modernizers' who edited *Hymns Ancient and Modern* (1861) and *The English Hymnal* (1906). Maxtone-Graham is right to detect a certain self-indulgently infantile nostalgia in the rearguard position: 'part of the reason hymn lovers feel so threatened by the seepage of evangelical songs into Anglican worship is that they think their childhood is being tampered with.'

But the fact remains that the late 20th century's new hymns don't stir any deeper emotion in me. They may make people feel comfortable and their catchiness usually leads to a rise in the decibel level, but they seek to connect to earth rather than heaven, preaching a gospel that doesn't look beyond friendliness and familiarity and social improvement. They do not minister to awe and wonder – the part of Christianity which passeth understanding, the sheer mystery of it.

So you will not find such hymns here; this is a book for those who sympathies and sensibilities are conservative; for those whose love hard pews, stained-glass windows, Early Perpendicular with Victorian additions, the gloriously resonant majesty of Cranmer's liturgy and the King James Bible; for those who go to church to lift up their hearts and sing, be it in or out of tune, through a screeching soprano, booming contralto, growling baritone or thunderous bass.

There aren't many of you now – the norm of congregational singing in the Church of England has become the sort of feeble drone, like the groans of dying beasts, that my headmaster rightly objected to, pathetic evidence of our culture's embarrassment at the expression of profound emotion focused on anything beyond the self. So stand up, take a deep breath, open your lungs – and let's hear it, 'once more, with feeling'.

A Brief History of the Hymn

'A good hymn is the most difficult thing in the world to write. In a good hymn you have to be both commonplace and poetical.'

Alfred, Lord Tennyson

Singing may be among the most primitive forms of religious worship, and Christian rituals and offices have almost always involved some musical setting of the liturgy or scripture. However, the modern concept of congregational hymn-singing is broadly speaking an innovation of the early German phase of the Reformation, during which Martin Luther himself wrote several great lyrics freely adapted from the psalms – the most famous example being the robust 'Ein' feste Burg ist unser Gott' (familiarly translated as 'A Safe Stronghold our God is still' or 'A Mighty Fortress is our God'), which springs from Psalm 46. Luther's hymns were designed to be sung, loudly and forthrightly, to familiar folk-tunes and they became the glue of the new Evangelism that was to sweep through Middle Europe. In England, however, the more cautious spirit of Anglicanism preferred the congregation to sing only strict metrical translations of psalms, chants and responses, contained in a volume known as Sternhold and Hopkins, while the richer glories of ecclesiastical music – notably Tallis and Byrd's sublime corpus of anthems and motets – were reserved to the choir.

The institution of a musical élite, however beautiful the sounds it made, was always problematic for a church founded in the idea of every believer's unmediated access to the godhead. The more militant nonconformists were having none of it: some sects (such as the Quakers) decided that singing was idolatrous and called for universal silence instead, but others let their vocal cords rip ecstatically. Two great figures dominate this phase of hymnody. Isaac Watts (1674-1748), a Congregationalist preacher more engaged by the human Jesus of the New Testament than the invisible God of the Old, ranks high in the annals of English literature as a religious poet, and his 1707 volume of *Hymns and Spiritual Songs* is the first significant hymn-book in the language. Inspired by what he heard of the exultant Moravian Brethren in America, John Wesley made mass open-air hymn singing a cornerstone of Methodism in the mid 18th century, using the vividly personal and fervent texts written by his prolific brother Charles Wesley (1707-88).

The Church of England was made anxious by the success of this tactic at bringing the love of Jesus direct to people's hearts through fresh poetry and melody. The psalm singing in its own churches came to seem drearily mechanical and slow in comparison: often it would consist of a chorister or Precentor singing a single line or phrase which would then be repeated by the (mostly illiterate) congregation. The only other music would be provided by a small choir singing the anthem from a gallery, accompanied by the sort of village band which Thomas Hardy affectionately mocks and celebrates in his novel *Under the Greenwood Tree*.

In the late 18th century, vicars on the Evangelical wing of Anglicanism began writing hymns for use in their parishes, though it was not until 1821 that the Synod of the Church of England officially sanctioned this practice. Their idea was to enliven worship by involving the whole congregation in the Lutheran style, energising them with rousing tunes and inspirational verse, basing texts on biblical sources.

From the 1830s, scholars such as J M Neale in the Anglo-Catholic Oxford Movement also promoted the translation of ancient hymns and chants written in Latin. These were more liturgical and less personal than Evangelical hymns, which tended to focus on the visceral revelation to the individual of God's love and Christ's suffering. Alongside this conservative innovation went a concerted effort to improve musical standards – organs and harmoniums replaced the chaotic village bands, choirs were robed and rehearsed by trained choirmasters and the Society for Promoting Church Music was established in 1845.

Hymn-books became ubiquitous – as Ian Bradley explains, putting them together 'ranks alongside butterfly collecting and fossil hunting as a favourite pastime of Victorian country clergy.' Over 1,200 collections, embracing many theological positions, were published in the 19th century, the most significant being *Hymns Ancient and Modern*, which sold over four million copies in the seven years following its appearance in 1861.

What distinguished *Hymns A and M*, as it became affectionately known, was its ecumenical liberalism: it was put together by a committee of parish clergymen of both High and Low sensibilities and was designed to present a broadly based selection of hymns which transcended the petty differences of sect, dogma and opinion that had marked previous collections. At the same time, *Hymns A and M* attempted for the first time to provide a sort of standardization, by assigning tunes to each hymn – previously, this had been a random process, largely left to the discretion of each parish choirmaster.

The second half of the 19th century saw the hymn's high watermark, both in Britain and the USA. Women took to writing them in their thousands, and Sunday School children were specially catered for by the likes of Mrs C F Alexander's 'All things bright and beautiful'. But the result of this explosion of activity was an awful lot of very bad hymns, marred by Victorian sanctimoniousness. The Roman Catholic church began to encourage the singing of hymns in this period, too, though the practice has never been as central to its services as it has been in Protestantism.

At the beginning of the 20th century, Ralph Vaughan Williams and Percy Dearmer decided to evacuate the Victorian slush. In *The English Hymnal*, published in 1906, they applied disinterested scholarship to the establishment of authoritative texts and the elimination of religiose bombast, as well as drawing on beautiful traditional folk-tunes to replace the drearier dirges. Twenty years later, in the aftermath of the First World War, Dearmer went on to publish a more progressive, strictly non-sectarian collection *Songs of Praise*, aimed at engaging with the issues and dilemmas of the modern world. This became hugely popular in schools, and gave its name to the long-running BBC Sunday television series.

The latest significant phase of hymn-writing began in the 1960s, as the New English Bible and the revision of the liturgy modernised the language of Anglican Christianity. New verse reflected scientific advances and tunes exploited the rhythms and clichés of pop music. Which, if any, of such hymns will survive the test of time remains to be seen.

The USA has made distinctive contributions to the corpus of Anglican hymns. From the southern plantations came the 'spiritual' hymns of African-American slaves, first authoritatively collected in *Slave Songs of the United States*, published in 1867. Black gospel hymns from industrial northern towns are a 20th-century phenomenon, particularly prevalent among evangelical sects. But most of the American hymns which have worked their way into the Anglican repertory and feature in this collection are the work of New England Abolitionists, writing in the period both before and after the Civil War.

Carols have a separate history, inasmuch as many of

them derive from winter folk-songs and dances which have nothing to do with Christianity – the word 'carol' may ultimately derive from a Greek word 'choros', used to describe a ritual of collective singing and dancing. St Francis and the itinerant Franciscan friars were pioneers of specifically Christian Christmas hymns on the theme of the nativity. In England, many beautiful carols such as 'Adam lay y-bounden' and the Boar's Head Carol date from the 15th and 16th centuries; some of these were sung in church until the Reformation began its clampdown on anything which didn't conform to scripture.

During the Commonwealth, Oliver Cromwell went so far as to ban the singing of Christmas carols, and although this was a brief and largely futile gesture, they re-established themselves outside church rather than within, as an element of seasonal drunken carousing and wassailing. In the 1820s, the antiquarians Davies Gilbert and William Sandys began collecting and publishing the songs, and they gradually found their way back into church services, against the background of the Victorian development of a tradition of snowy Christmas cheer.

In the early 20th century, Ralph Vaughan Williams, Percy Dearmer and Cecil Sharp made scholarly editions of carols, and the choir of King's College, Cambridge began its celebrated Festival of Nine Lessons and Carols in 1918. This service, broadcast by the BBC, has since become recognised as the artistic pinnacle of Christmas music, imitated in some form in churches throughout the land. The humble old vernacular custom of lusty wassailing continues too, in charitable singalongs on station forecourts and in shopping malls, as well as door-to-door.

Hymns

1. *Abide with me*

A hymn much sung at funerals and cremations which, as Erik Routley put it, 'looks death itself in the face' and embodies the human craving for companionship in extremis. The text is the posthumously published work of Henry Francis Lyte (1793-1847), a neurotic and sickly curate who spent most of his pastoral career in the fishing village of Lower Brixham in Devon. He had been haunted by the phrase 'Abide with me' which he had heard repeatedly muttered by his close friend, William Le Hunte, as he lay dying, significantly misremembered from Luke 24:29, where the disciples meet but do not recognize the resurrected Jesus on the road to Emmaus. 'Abide with us,' they ask him, 'for it is toward evening, and the day is far spent.' As has often been remarked, the change to the singular pronoun is what gives the hymn its comforting emotional intimacy.

Lyte wrote 'Abide with me' to his own tune, but today it is always sung to 'Eventide', a melancholy melody composed in ten minutes by the organist William Monk, during what his widow later recalled as 'a time of great sorrow. Hand in hand we were silently watching the glory of the setting sun (our daily habit) until the golden hue had faded… Then he took paper and pencilled the tune which has gone all over the world.'

'Abide with me' was hugely popular in the trenches of the First World War, and was sung by Nurse Edith Cavell when the Anglican chaplain visited her in the condemned cell the night before the Germans shot her for helping British soldiers to escape from occupied Belgium.

A great favourite of the royal family, 'Abide with me' was selected for the wedding of the future George VI to Elizabeth Bowes-Lyon and of their daughter Elizabeth to Prince Philip. It has long remained a fixture of the FA Cup Final, Anzac Day and the British Legion's Festival of Remembrance at the Royal Albert Hall. On 21 September 2001 it was unforgettably played at Ground Zero by a Salvation Army band during the commemoration of the 9/11 attack. It also features on the soundtracks of several movies – *The Full Monty*, *28 Days Later*, *A Bridge Too Far* – invariably associated with mourning and tragedy.

Abide with me

Abide with me; fast falls the eventide:
The darkness deepens; Lord, with me abide:
When other helpers fail, and comforts flee,
Help of the helpless, O abide with me.

Swift to its close ebbs out life's little day;
Earth's joys grow dim, its glories pass away;
Change and decay in all around I see:
O thou who changest not, abide with me.

I need thy presence ev'ry passing hour;
What but thy grace can foil the tempter's power?
Who like thyself my guide and stay can be?
Through cloud and sunshine, Lord abide with me.

I fear no foe, with thee at hand to bless;
Ills have no weight, and tears no bitterness.
Where is death's sting? Where, grave, thy victory?
I triumph still, if thou abide with me.

Hold thou thy Cross before my closing eyes;
Shine through the gloom, and point me to the skies:
Heaven's morning breaks, and earth's vain shadows flee:
In life, in death, O Lord, abide with me.

2. *All creatures of our God and King*

Based on the *Canticle of Brother Sun* or *Canticle of the Creatures*, written in the early 13th century by St Francis of Assisi, supposedly during an ecstatic fit following his 40-night vigil in a rat-infested hut. The biblical inspiration is Psalm 148. This translation was made by the Tractarian rector W H Draper (1855-1933), omitting the Brother-Sister theme of Francis's original. 'Lasst uns erfreuen', the tune to which it is sung nowadays, first appeared in a 17th-century German collection, incorporated by Vaughan Williams into *The English Hymnal* (1906).

All creatures of our God and King,
Lift up your voice and with us sing
Alleluia, Alleluia!
Thou burning sun with golden beam
Thou silver moon with softer gleam,

Refrain : *O praise him, O Praise him,*
Alleluia, Alleluia, Alleluia!

Thou rushing wind that art so strong,
Ye clouds that sail in heaven along,
O praise him, Alleluia!
Thou rising morn in praise, rejoice,
Ye lights of evening, find a voice;

Thou flowing water, pure and clear,
Make music for thy Lord to hear
Alleluia, Alleluia!
Thou fire so masterful and bright,
That givest man both warmth and light:

And all ye men of tender heart,
Forgiving others, take your part,
O sing ye, Alleluia!
Ye who long pain and sorrow bear,
Praise God and on him cast your care:

Let all things their Creator bless
And worship him in humbleness,
O praise him, Alleluia!
Praise, praise the Father, praise the Son,
And praise the Spirit, Three in One.

3. *All people that on earth do dwell*

One of the oldest hymns to be regularly sung in churches today, this adaptation of Psalm 100 was probably written by a Scottish friend of John Knox called William Kethe (ob. 1594), a Calvinist exile in Geneva during the reign of Bloody Mary (1553-8). The robust tune 'Old Hundredth' has been dated back to a psalter of 1560 and seems to have been the work of the French composer Louis Bourgeois.

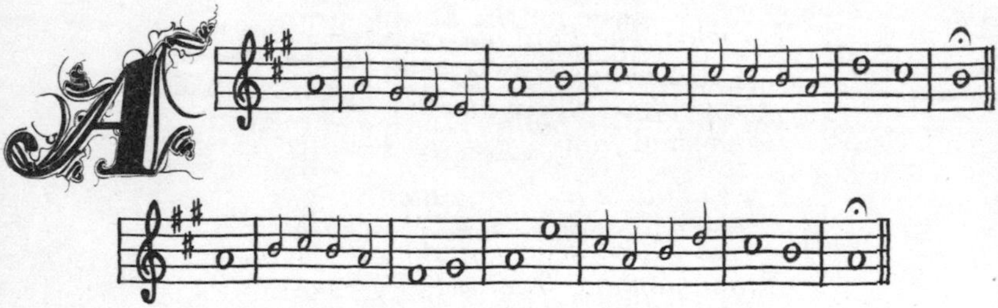

All people that on earth do dwell,
Sing to the Lord with cheerful voice;
Him serve with fear, his praise forth tell,
Come ye before him, and rejoice.

The Lord, ye know, is God indeed;
Without our aid he did us make;
We are his folk, he doth us feed,
And for his sheep he doth us take.

O enter then his gates with praise,
Approach with joy his courts unto;
Praise, laud, and bless his name always,
For it is seemly so to do.

For why? The Lord our God is good;
His mercy is for ever sure;
His truth at all times firmly stood,
And shall from age to age endure.

To Father, Son and Holy Ghost,
The God whom heaven and earth adore,
From men and from the angel-host
Be praise and glory evermore.

4. *All things bright and beautiful*

This hugely popular but faintly nauseating 'little' Sunday School hymn for infants was first published in 1848, in a collection of hymns designed to raise money for deaf-mutes.

It was written by Mrs Cecil Frances Alexander (1818-95), wife of the Archbishop of Armagh and Protestant Primate of Ireland, as a way of elucidating the opening of the Apostles' Creed: 'I believe in God, the Father Almighty, Maker of heaven and earth.' A member of the Anglo-Irish establishment, Mrs Alexander clearly had no compunction about keeping the rich man in his castle and the poor man at his gate, but even before the age of political correctness, the offending third verse was usually omitted – the Inner London Education Authority positively banned it in 1982. Mrs Alexander's defenders suggest that what she meant to imply was the inclusiveness of God's creative power, rather than his sanctioning of a social hierarchy.

James Herriot used the second line of the refrain as the title for his book about the adventures of a young Yorkshire vet and his eccentric partner Siegfried Farnon, later adapted into a popular BBC television series.

The cheerfully swinging tune 'Royal Oak' was arranged by Martin Shaw in 1915 from a traditional melody celebrating the restoration of Charles II in 1660. Schools often use a simplified version by William Henry Monk.

All things bright and beautiful

Refrain : *All things bright and beautiful,*
All creatures great and small,
All things wise and wonderful,
The Lord God made them all.

Each little flower that opens,
Each little bird that sings.
He made their glowing colours,
He made their tiny wings.

The rich man in his castle,
The poor man at his gate,
God made them, high or lowly,
And ordered their estate.

The purple-headed mountain,
The river running by,
The sunset and the morning,
That brightens up the sky;

The cold wind in the winter,
The pleasant summer sun,
The ripe fruits in the garden
He made them every one;

The tall trees in the greenwood
The meadows for our play,
That rushes by the water
To gather every day;

He gave us eyes to see them,
And lips that we may tell
How great is God Almighty,
Who has made all things well.

5. *Alleluia, sing to Jesus!*

The hymnologist Percy Dearmer was rather snooty about this stirring piece of Victorian high churchism. 'It makes up in heartiness what it lacks in beauty and intellectual power,' he wrote. Other authorities, however, have admired its rich texture of scriptural allusion. It was written in 1866 by a Bristolian insurance agent William C Dix (1837-98), who also wrote the Epiphany hymn 'As with gladness men of old'. The tune is 'Hyfrydol', composed in 1844 by the 20-year old Rowland Prichard, a loom-tender for the Welsh Flannel Manufacturing Company – see also 'Love divine, all loves excelling'.

Alleluia, sing to Jesus!
His the sceptre, his the throne;
Alleluia! His the triumph,
His the victory alone:
Hark! The songs of peaceful Zion
Thunder like a mighty flood;
Jesus, out of every nation,
Hath redeemed us by his blood.

Alleluia, not as orphans
Are we left in sorrow now;
Alleluia! He is near us,
Faith believes, nor questions how;
Though the cloud from sight received him
When the forty days were o'er,
Shall our hearts forget his promise,
'I am with you evermore'?

Alleluia, bread of angels,
Thou on earth our food, our stay;
Alleluia! Here the sinful
Flee to thee from day to day:
Intercessor, friend of sinners,
Earth's redeemer, plead for me,
Where the songs of all the sinless
Sweep across the crystal sea.

Alleluia, King eternal,
Thee the Lord of lords we own;
Alleluia! born of Mary,
Earth thy footstool, heav'n thy throne:
Thou within the veil has entered,
Robed in flesh, our great High Priest;
Thou on earth both priest and victim
In the Eucharistic feast.

6. *Amazing Grace*

'Faith's Review and Expectation' is what its author John Newton (1725-1807) entitled this hymn when it was first published in 1779. Newton's life-story is a dramatic one by the sedate standards of hymn-writers, and his quest for that faith was long and tortuous.

The son of a sailor, he was sent to sea at the age of eleven, after only minimal schooling. Some years later, having fallen madly in love, he deserted his ship, only to be press-ganged back into service, then flogged and chained and reduced to the lowest rank. He deserted again, ending up on the coast of what is now Sierra Leone, where he worked for a planter who treated him little better than a slave. As he degenerated morally, the only vestige of civilization he maintained was a dog-eared book of Euclidean geometry, figures from which he carved into the sand by moonlight.

A letter from his father made him decide to return to England in 1748. A violent storm on the route home nearly wrecked his ship and reminded him of the value of the religion he had learnt in childhood. He cleaned himself up, embarked on a programme of classical self-education and joined the slave trade, eventually rising to Captain. The rational Anglicanism of the age didn't fully engage his restless spirit, however, and it was only in 1754, when he became friendly with John Wesley and discovered the Evangelical movement, that he finally surrendered 'every energy of his mind and body' to God.

For some years, he continued in the slave trade – the ethics of which didn't seem to bother him unduly – but eventually he was ordained, and in 1764 he became the hugely popular and tireless curate of Olney in Buckinghamshire, where his change of heart led him to associate himself with William Wilberforce's campaign for the abolition of slavery. He remained in the Olney living for seventeen years and became friendly with his neighbour, the depressive poet William Cowper. Together they edited a three-volume collection, *Olney Hymns*, much of which they also wrote themselves. It was here that 'Amazing Grace' first appeared.

For nearly two centuries, the hymn was not widely sung, although it was always better known in the United States than in Britain – in 1831, an American hymn-book called Virginia Harmony attached it to a pentatonic Scots-American bagpipe tune, 'New Britain', and the two have remained indelibly linked ever since.

But in the last fifty years or so, it has become a black gospel song, and an unofficial anthem of the Civil Rights movement as well as many other humanitarian causes (including the ever-increasing cohorts of those on the pilgrimage of rehab). Today, its status is even higher: as the seeming embodiment of the spiritual heart of America, it has become a call to national seriousness, often sung at solemn occasions, such as the commemorations of 9/11 and Hurricane Katrina.

It's not easy to date or explain this process, though the hymn did feature prominently in *Alice's Restaurant*, Arthur Penn's 1969 movie about the counter-culture and Vietnam draft-dodging.

In Britain the following year, a recording by the pipes and drums of the Royal Scots and Dragoons topped the pops. Since then, the hymn has also shown up in several other films – *Star Trek* 2, *Silkwood*, *Betrayed* and *The Last Days of Disco* among them – and been covered by a remarkable variety of singers, from Elvis Presley to Aretha Franklin to Rod Stewart, Dolly Parton and Christina Aguilera.

In 2007, Albert Finney played John Newton in a dull but worthy film about the abolition of slavery called *Amazing Grace*.

Amazing Grace! How sweet the sound
That saved a wretch like me!
I once was lost, but now am found,
Was blind, but now I see.

'Twas grace that taught my heart to fear,
And grace my fears relieved;
How precious did that grace appear
The hour I first believed.

Through many dangers, toils and snares
I have already come.
'Tis grace hath brought me safe thus far,
And grace will lead me home.

The Lord has promised good to me,
His word my hope secures;
He will my shield and portion be
As long as life endures.

When we've been there a thousand years,
Bright shining as the sun,
We've no less days to sing God's praise
Than when we first began.

7. And did those feet in ancient time

It was the Poet Laureate Robert Bridges who in 1916 first extracted these verses from the preface to the 'prophetic book' Milton (1800-4) by William Blake (1757-1827) for inclusion in a patriotic anthology entitled *The Spirit of Man*. Hubert Parry was then asked to provide a tune, so that it could be sung as a hymn at meetings of 'Fight for Right' a charitable crusade aimed at helping soldiers rehabilitate themselves. Elgar made the orchestral arrangement.

In 1918 'Jerusalem' was sung at a rally at the Royal Albert Hall celebrating the extension of female suffrage, and was subsequently adopted by the Women's Institute. Since the Second World War, it has also been sung regularly at the Last Night of the Proms and at Labour Party conferences. Of the many competitive sporting events with which it has been associated, the 2005 Ashes stands out, with the sponsors, npower, attempting to organize a nationwide sing-in five minutes before the start of the final Test at the Oval. This did not come off, but the victorious England team went on to record the hymn, led by the 'pop sensation' Keedie.

Is 'Jerusalem' now more one of two unofficial British – or English – national anthems (the other being 'Land of Hope and Glory') than a sacred hymn?

For all the spine-tingling magnificence of its mystical imagery, its roots are not in the Bible so much as the (unfounded) legend that Jesus wandered into Britain in the company of Joseph of Arimethea and visited Cornwall and Glastonbury. Whatever the myth, it now represents an acceptable face of nationalist aspiration and like 'Amazing Grace' in the US, it is probably sung more often outside churches than inside them. Several Anglican hymn-books pointedly exclude it.

Among the many rock and pop cover versions are those by Billy Bragg, Emerson, Lake and Palmer and The Fall. It can also be heard in several movies including *The Loneliness of the Long-Distance Runner*, *Chariots of Fire* (with throbbing Vangelis overlay) and *Four Weddings and a Funeral*, as well as episodes of television series such as *Monty Python's Flying Circus*, *Star Trek* and *Shameless.*

And did those feet in ancient time

And did those feet in ancient time
Walk upon England's mountains green?
And was the holy Lamb of God
On England's pleasant pastures seen?
And did the countenance divine
Shine forth upon our clouded hills?
And was Jerusalem builded here
Among those dark satanic mills?

Bring me my bow of burning gold!
Bring me my arrows of desire!
Bring me my spear! O clouds, unfold!
Bring me my chariot of fire!
I will not cease from mental fight
Nor shall my sword sleep in my hand
Till we have built Jerusalem
In England's green and pleasant land.

8. *At the name of Jesus*

According to Emma Pitman, Caroline Maria Noel (1817-77) 'learned in suffering what she taught in song'. A frail Victorian spinster, she endured 'a long illness of twenty years before the end came' and spent much of her life recumbent on the sofa. Her hymnal entitled *The Name of Jesus*, in which this uplifting verse stood out, was written most emphatically for the 'sick and lonely.' The jaunty tune, 'Camberwell', is by Michael Brierley.

At the name of Jesus
Every knee shall bow,
Every tongue confess him
King of glory now;
'Tis the Father's pleasure
We should call him Lord,
Who from the beginning
Was the mighty word.

Humbled for a season,
To receive a name
From the lips of sinners
Unto whom he came,
Faithfully he bore it
Spotless to the last,
Brought it back victorious
When from death he passed.

Bore it up triumphant
With its human light,
Through all ranks of creatures,
To the central height,
To the throne of Godhead,
To the Father's breast;
Filled it with the glory
Of that perfect rest.

Name him, brothers, name him,
With love as strong as death,
But with awe and wonder,
And with bated breath;
He is God the Saviour,
He is Christ the Lord
Ever to be worshipped,
Trusted, and adored.

9. *Blest are the pure in heart*

Based on the sixth beatitude from the Sermon on the Mount (Matthew 5:8), this was cobbled together for a hymn-book published in 1836. The first and third verses are by John Keble (1792-1866), drawn from a poem he wrote for private meditation rather than public singing in *The Christian Year*; the second and fourth verses are by W J Hall and E Osler.

The tune 'Franconia' is derived from an 18th-century German melody.

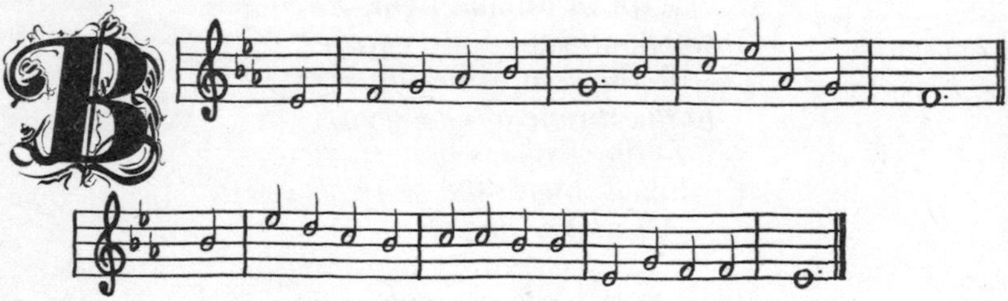

Blest are the pure in heart,
For they shall see our God;
The secret of the Lord is theirs,
Their soul is Christ's abode.

The Lord, who left the heavens
Our life and peace to bring,
To dwell in lowliness with men,
Their pattern and their King.

He to the lowly soul
Doth still himself impart;
And for his dwelling and his throne
Chooseth the pure in heart.

Lord, we thy presence seek;
May ours this blessing be;
Give us a pure and lowly heart,
A temple meet for thee.

10. *Breathe on me, Breath of God*

It was said of his religion that 'it was as simple and unaffected as a child's,' records Ian Bradley in writing about the author of this hymn, Dr Edwin Hatch (1835-89), an ecclesiastical historian at Oxford University, friendly with the Pre-Raphaelite Brotherhood. In 1878 he published this invocation to the Holy Ghost in a pamphlet called *Between Doubt and Prayer*.

Of the many tunes to which it has been sung, 'Carlisle', composed by the blind Charles Lockhart, is probably the most familiar.

Breathe on me, Breath of God,
Fill me with life anew,
That I may love what thou dost love,
And do what thou wouldst do.

Breathe on me, Breath of God,
Until my heart is pure,
Until with thee I will one will.
To do and to endure.

Breathe on me, Breath of God,
Blend all my soul with thine,
Until this earthly part of me
Glows with thy fire divine.

Breathe on me, Breath of god;
So shall I never die,
But live with thee the perfect life
Of thine eternity.

11. Christ is made the sure foundation

The second part of an early medieval hymn called 'The Blessed City of Jerusalem', translated and adapted by J M Neale (1818-66) from a monastic hymnbook. It was inspired by Paul's letter to the Ephesians 2:20-1, which describes the 'household of God' as 'built upon the foundation of the apostles and prophets, Jesus Christ himself being the chief corner-stone; in whom all the building fitly framed together groweth unto an holy temple in the Lord.'

Its tune 'Westminster Abbey' is adapted from an anthem by Henry Purcell.

Christ is made the sure foundation,
Christ the Head and Corner-stone,
Chosen of the Lord, and precious,
Binding all the Church in one,
Holy Zion's help for ever,
And her confidence alone.

All that dedicated city,
Dearly loved of God on high,
In exultant jubilation,
Pours perpetual melody,
God the One in Three adoring
In glad hymns eternally.

To this temple, where we call thee,
Come, o Lord of Hosts, today;
With thy wonted loving-kindness
Hear thy servants as they pray;
And thy fullest benediction
Shed within its walls alway.

Here vouchsafe to all thy servants,
What they ask of thee to gain,
What they gain from thee for ever
With the blessed to retain,
And hereafter in the glory
Evermore with thee to reign.

Laud and honour to the Father,
Laud and honour to the Son,
Laud and honour to the Spirit;
Ever Three and ever One;
Consubstantial, co-eternal,
While unending ages run.

12. *Dear Lord and Father of mankind*

Ironically, the author of this movingly beautiful and much-loved hymn deeply disapproved of singing in church. John Greenleaf Whittier (1807-92) was an American Quaker, who firmly believed that God was best worshipped in silent meditation and who deplored the histrionics associated with both the High Church and the Evangelical movement.

But he did allow the verses to be used in a hymn-book published in 1884. They are drawn from an interlude in his long and eccentric poem called *The Brewing of Soma*, which describes in shocked terms the Vedic Hindu habit of drinking hallucinogenic concoctions as a way of whipping up religious enthusiasm. Whittier advocated waiting instead for 'the still small voice of calm' – an injunction beautifully suggested in the climax to its tune 'Repton', composed by Hubert Parry as an adaptation of an aria, 'Long since in Egypt's plenteous land', which appears in his oratorio of *1888 Judith*.

HYMNS
167
260

Dear Lord and Father of mankind

Dear Lord and Father of mankind,
Forgive our foolish ways!
Re-clothe us in our rightful mind
In purer lives thy service find,
In deeper reverence praise.

In simple trust like theirs who heard,
Beside the Syrian sea,
The gracious calling of the Lord,
Let us, like them, without a word
Rise up and follow thee.

O Sabbath rest by Galilee!
O calm of hills above,
Where Jesus knelt to share with thee
The silence of eternity,
Interpreted by love!

With that deep hush subduing all
Our words and works that drown
The tender whisper of thy call,
As noiseless let thy blessing fall
As fell thy manna down.

Drop thy still dews of quietness
Till all our strivings cease;
Take from our souls the strain and stress,
And let our ordered lives confess
The beauty of thy peace.

Breathe through the heats of our desire
Thy coolness and thy balm;
Let sense be dumb, let flesh retire;
Speak through the earthquake, wind and fire,
O still small voice of calm!

13. Eternal Father, strong to save

Known as 'the Sailors' hymn' and adopted as the anthem of both the British and American navies, addressing in successive verses the Trinity of Father, Son and Holy Ghost, it was written in several versions through the 1860s, by William Whiting (1825-78), choirmaster of Winchester College. Legend suggests that it was conceived as a gift to an anxious choirboy about to set sail for America.

Winston Churchill ordered it to be sung on the HMS Prince of Wales when he had his fateful mid-Atlantic meeting with Franklin D Roosevelt during the Second World War, and it was often heard during the Falklands War of 1982. It was sung at the funerals of Roosevelt, John F. Kennedy, Ronald Reagan and Gerald Ford. It features in several movies including *Crimson Tide*, *The Right Stuff*, *The Perfect Storm* and *Titanic*.

In 1915, new verses were added for the age of air travel

Lord, guard and guide the men who fly
Through the great spaces in the sky.
Be with them always in the air,
In darkening storms or sunlight fair;
Oh, hear us when we lift our prayer,
For those in peril in the air!

but they lack the stirring Miltonic grandeur of Whiting's original, as do subsequent additions made for marines, seabees, merchant marines, coastguards, divers and submariners, naval nurses, Antarctic and Arctic servicemen, space travellers, those wounded in combat, and civilians at home.

The tune 'Melita' (or Malta, after the place of St Paul's shipwreck in Acts 28:1), with its wonderful swell and ebb at the end of the verse, was the work of the leading Victorian hymn composer, J B Dykes, who contributed fifty-six tunes to the 1875 edition of *Hymns Ancient and Modern*. This setting is unforgettably featured as one of the congregational hymns in Benjamin Britten's community opera *Noye's Fludde* (1957), counterpointed by a splendid battery of percussive storm music.

Eternal Father, strong to save

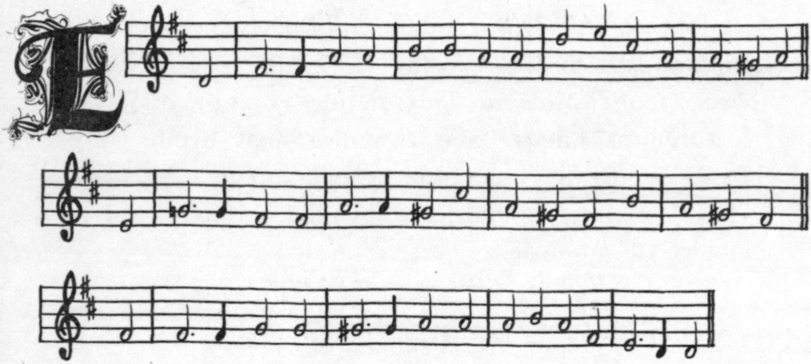

Eternal Father, strong to save,
Whose arm hath bound the restless wave,
Who bidd'st the mighty ocean deep
Its own appointed limits keep:
O hear us when we cry to thee,
For those in peril on the sea.

O Christ, whose voice the waters heard
And hushed their raging at thy word,
Who walkedst on the foaming deep
And calm amid its storm didst sleep;
O hear us when we cry to thee
For those in peril on the sea.

O holy Spirit, who didst brood
Upon the waters dark and rude,
And bid their angry tumult cease
And give, for wild confusion, peace:
O hear us when we cry to thee
For those in peril on the sea.

O Trinity of love and power,
Our brethren shield in danger's hour,
From rock and tempest, fire and foe,
Protect them wheresoe'er they go:
Thus evermore shall rise to thee
Glad hymns of praise from land and sea.

14. *Fight the good fight*

In I Timothy 6:12, Paul instructs the faithful to 'fight the good fight of faith, lay hold of eternal life, whereunto thou art also called.' In 1863 this stirring sentiment was used as the basis for a hymn by the vicar of Egham, John Monsell (1811-75) – 'a decidedly second-rate hymn writer' complained Erik Routley. However, he went on to point out that 'just as Paul uncannily combined a hard-headed realism with a profound and tender devotion, so this hymn combines a mystical Christ-centredness with its bold and homely injunctions.'

It's a testosterone-charged hymn, designed for males to sing loudly and lustily: Susan Tamke claims that 'it speaks the language of the public school boy: competition, fighting, racing, winning prizes' – and as such it has long been a staple of religious services in such institutions.

The tune is 'Duke Street', attributed to John Hatton.

Fight the good fight with all thy might
Christ is thy strength and Christ thy right
Lay hold on life, and it shall be
Thy joy and crown eternally.

Run the straight race through God's good grace,
Lift up thine eyes and seek his face;
Life with its way before us lies,
Christ is the path and Christ the prize.

Cast care aside; upon thy Guide
Lean, and his mercy will provide.
Lean, and the trusting soul shall prove
Christ is its life, and Christ its love.

Faint not nor fear, his arms are near;
He changeth not and thou art dear;
Only believe, and thou shalt see
That Christ is all in all to thee.

15. *Firmly I believe and truly*

From *The Dream of Gerontius* (1865), a long dramatic poem by John Henry Newman (1801-90), set as an oratorio by Elgar in 1900 and turned into a hymn six years later for *The English Hymnal*. Newman charts the spiritual journey of an elderly monk who dies and goes to meet his maker. The theme, in the words of J R Watson, is 'the assurance of the Roman Catholic church as a safeguard against the perplexing transiences of the age.' Despite this bent, the hymn has been adopted into Anglicanism, although strict Protestants often exclude the last verse, with its theologically contentious reference to the agency of the angelic host.

Firmly I believe and truly

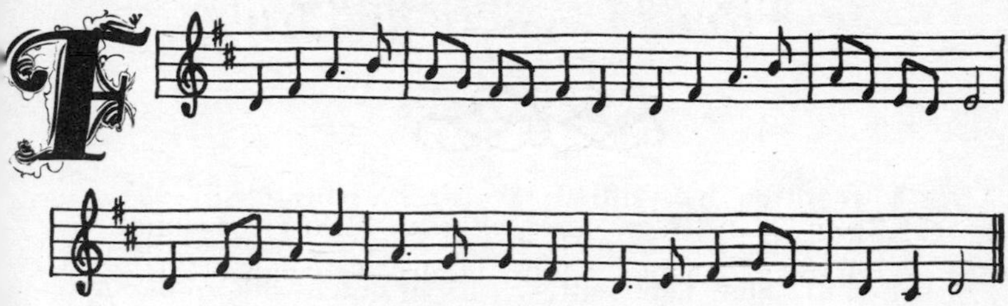

Firmly I believe and truly
God is Three, and God is One;
And I next acknowledge duly
Manhood taken by the Son.

And I trust and hope most fully
In that Manhood crucified;
And each thought and deed unruly
Do to death, as he has died.

Simply to his grace and wholly
Light and life and strength belong.
And I love supremely, solely,
Him the Holy, him the Strong.

And I hold in veneration,
For the love of him alone,
Holy Church is his creation,
And her teachings as his own.

Adoration aye be given,
With and through the angelic host,
To the God of earth and heaven
Father, Son and Holy Ghost.

16. *For all the Saints*

Written by William Walsham How (1823-97) while he was a Rector in Shropshire and published in 1864. Later, after years of good work among the poor in the East End, How was consecrated Bishop of Wakefield and became affectionately known as 'the omnibus Bishop', in reference to his preference for travelling by public transport.

J R Watson calls it 'a very splendid hymn with the kind of imagery of power and battles that Tolkien was later to use in *The Lord of the Rings*'. The tune is 'Sine Nomine', composed by Vaughan Williams for *The English Hymnal* (1906).

For all the Saints who from their labours rest,
Who thee by faith before the world confessed,
Thy name, O Jesus, be for ever blest. Alleluia!

Thou wast their Rock, their Fortress, and their Might;
Thou, Lord, their Captain in the well-fought fight
Thou, in the darkness drear, their one true Light.
Alleluia!

O may thy soldiers, faithful, true and bold,
Fight as the Saints who nobly fought of old,
And win, with them, the victor's crown of gold.
Alleluia!

O blest communion, fellowship divine!
We feebly struggle, they in glory shine;
Yet all are one in thee, for all are thine. Alleluia!

And when the strife is fierce, the warfare long,
Steals on the ear the distant triumph song,
And hearts are brave again, and arms are strong.
Alleluia!

The golden evening brightens in the west;
Soon, soon to faithful warriors cometh rest;
Sweet is the calm of Paradise the blest. Alleluia!

But, lo! There breaks a yet more glorious day;
The Saints triumphant rise in bright array;
The King of glory passes on his way. Alleluia!

From earth's wide bounds, from ocean's farthest coast,
Through gates of pearl streams in the countless host,
Singing to Father, Son and Holy Ghost. Alleluia!

17. *Glorious things of thee are spoken*

Along with 'Amazing Grace', this is the most famous hymn written by the born-again slave trader John Newton (1725-1807), the text drawing its imagery from a rich variety of scriptural sources in Exodus, the Psalms, Isaiah and Revelation.

The tune 'Austria' is Joseph Haydn's arrangement of a Croatian folk song. He composed it in 1797, for the birthday of the Habsburg Emperor Francis II – 'Gott, erhalte Franz den Kaiser'. Haydn subsequently used the tune as the theme for the slow movement of his 'Emperor' String Quartet, and it served as the imperial anthem until 1919. (In 1922, the Weimar Republic adopted it as the German National Anthem, using the title 'Deutschland, über Alles'; the Nazis followed suit, playing it alongside their party anthem, 'the Horst-Wessel Lied'. Since 1952, Germany has dropped 'Deutschland, über Alles', because of its supremacist implications, and now Haydn's gracious tune is sung to a verse beginning 'Einigkeit und Recht und Freiheit', 'Unity and Law and Freedom'.)

Glorious things of thee are spoken

Glorious things of thee are spoken,
Zion, city of our God!
He whose word cannot be broken
Formed thee for his own abode:
On the Rock of Ages founded,
What can shake thy sure repose?
With salvation's walls surrounded,
Thou may'st smile at all thy foes.

See, the streams of living waters,
Springing from eternal love,
Well supply thy sons and daughters,
And all fear of want remove:
Who can faint while such a river
Ever flows their thirst to assuage?
Grace, which like the Lord the Giver,
Never fails from age to age.

Saviour, if of Zion's city
I, through grace, a member am,
Let the world deride or pity,
I will glory in thy name:
Fading is the worldling's pleasure,
All his boasted pomp and show;
Solid joys and lasting treasure
None but Zion's children know.

18. God is working his purpose out

Arthur Ainger (1841-1919) was a classics master at Eton who 'reserved admirable and friendly discipline by means of a dry and ready irony ... his justice, courtesy and unruffled good humour won the respect and admiration of the boys.'

This agreeable figure wrote this inspiringly upbeat hymn in 1894, at the height of the British imperial adventure, dedicating it to his friend E W Benson, the Archbishop of Canterbury. The idea of the waters covering the sea may strike one as absurd – aren't they wet enough already? – but the image is drawn from Habbakuk 2:14: 'For the earth shall be filled with the knowledge of the glory of the Lord, as the waters cover the sea.'

The tune 'Benson' was composed in 1894 by the otherwise obscure village organist Millicent Kingham.

God is working his purpose out

God is working his purpose out as year succeeds to year;
God is working his purpose out and the time is drawing near;
Nearer and nearer draws the time, the time that shall surely be,
When the earth shall be filled with the glory of God as the waters cover the sea.

From utmost east to utmost west where e'er man's foot hath trod,
By the mouth of many messengers goes forth the voice of God,
'Give ear to me, ye continents, ye isles, give ear to me,
That the earth may be filled with the glory of God as the waters cover the sea.'

What can we do to work God's work, to prosper and increase
The brotherhood of all mankind, the reign of the Prince of Peace?
What can we do hasten the time, the time that shall surely be,
When the earth shall be filled with the glory of God as the waters cover the sea?

March we forth in the strength of God with the banner of Christ unfurled,
That the light of the glorious gospel of truth may shine throughout the world;
Fight we the fight with sorrow and sin, to set their captives free.
That the earth may be filled with the glory of God as the waters cover the sea.

All we can do is nothing worth unless God blesses the deed;
Vainly we hope for the harvest tide till God gives life to the seed;
Yet nearer and nearer draws the time, the time that shall surely be,
When the earth shall be filled with the glory of God as the waters cover the sea.

19. *Guide me, O thou great Jehovah*

Indelibly associated with Welsh Male Voice Choirs and Eisteddfods, this hymn was originally written in Welsh by a Methodist preacher William Williams (1719-91), a pioneering hymnist who (in the words of S W Duffield) 'did for Wales what Wesley and Watts did for England.' In 1771 it was translated into English by Peter Williams, no relation, and Williams himself. The verse was tinkered with several times in the course of the 19th century, and the hymn is still often sung as 'Guide me, o thou great Redeemer'. It can be heard sung in Welsh in John Ford's Oscar-winning movie of 1941, *How Green was my Valley*.

Williams' words have been much admired for their plain yet majestic dignity. 'The grandest re-enactment in modern hymnody of the Israelite journey through the barren wilderness to the Promised Land, which is the type of all spiritual pilgrimage', assert Marjorie Reeves and Jenyth Worsley; while J R Watson judges it 'one of the greatest of evangelical hymns, mainly because of its understatement.'

The tune, 'Cwm Rhondda', sung in the trenches and mines as well as at numberless rugby matches, was composed in 1905 by John Hughes for a singing festival – legend has it that he wrote it in chalk on a tarpaulin (though why he should have done so has never been explained). The repeated high notes of the verse's last line are a gift to Welsh tenors keen to show off their larynxes and can be drawn out to awesomely vulgar musical effect.

The hymn was sung at the Princess of Wales' funeral in 1997.

Guide me, O thou great Jehovah

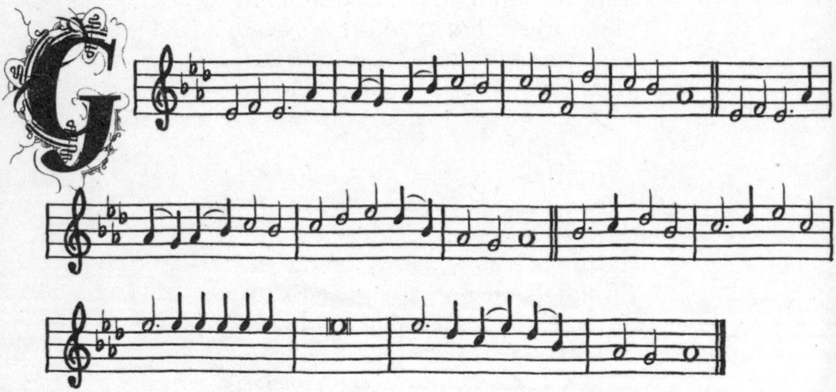

Guide me, O thou great Jehovah,
Pilgrim through this barren land;
I am weak, but thou art mighty;
Hold me with thy powerful hand;
Bread of heaven, bread of heaven,
Feed me till I want no more.

Open now the crystal fountain,
Whence the healing stream doth flow;
Let the fire and cloudy pillar
Lead me all my journey through;
Strong Deliv'rer, strong Deliv'rer,
Be thou still my strength and shield

When I tread the verge of Jordan
Bid my anxious fears subside;
Death of death, and hell's destruction,
Land me safe on Canaan's side;
Songs of praises, songs of praises,
I will ever give to thee.

20. *Holy, Holy, Holy*

Thackeray called Reginald Heber (1783-1826) 'one of the good knights of the time and one of the best of English gentlemen'. Later in his poignantly short career he became Bishop of Calcutta, but he was a cultured Anglican vicar in Shropshire when he wrote this posthumously published hymn. The inspiration was Revelation 4:8, in which four beasts with six wings 'full of eyes within… rest not day and night, saying Holy, Holy, Holy, Lord God Almighty, which was, and is, and is to come.'

Tennyson much admired this hymn, as did the theologian Erik Routley, who reflected that 'the very shakiness and disjointedness in the hymn are a kind of humility. What we think is of less importance than what God is.'

The tune 'Nicaea' is by J B Dykes, composed for *Hymns Ancient and Modern* in 1861. The Council of Nicaea in 325 defined the doctrine of the Trinity, making it an appropriate reference to a hymn designed to be sung on Trinity Sunday.

Holy, Holy, Holy!

Holy, holy, holy! Lord God Almighty!
Early in the morning our song shall rise to thee;
Holy, holy, holy! merciful and mighty!
God in three persons, blessed Trinity!

Holy, holy, holy! All the saints adore thee,
Casting down their golden crowns around the glassy sea,
Cherubim and seraphim, falling down before thee,
Which wert, and art, and ever more shalt be.

Holy, holy, holy! Though the darkness hide thee,
Though the eye of sinful man thy glory may not see,
Only thou art holy; there is none beside thee,
Perfect in power, in love and purity.

Holy, holy, holy! Lord God Almighty!
All thy works shall praise thy name in earth and sky and sea;
Holy, holy, holy! Merciful and mighty!
God in three persons, blessed Trinity!

21. *I vow to thee, my country*

Such is the emotional patriotism in this hymn that Kipling is often supposed to have written it, but in fact it is the work of an Edwardian diplomat Sir Cecil Spring-Rice (1859-1918). It was sung at both the wedding and the funeral of Diana Princess of Wales – she said it had 'always been a favourite since schooldays'.

Spring-Rice's unfashionable sentiments have often worried the more progressive wing of the Church of England. In 2001, a vicar in Manchester refused to allow the hymn to be sung at a wedding, and it was attacked in 2004 by Stephen Lowe, Bishop of Hulme: 'While I am proud to be English,' he wrote, 'it is dangerous for a nation to suggest that our culture is somehow superior to others.'

The tune 'Thaxted' is by Gustav Holst, taken from the 'Jupiter, Bringer of Jollity' movement of his orchestral suite *The Planets* – the connection being made by Spring-Rice's daughter, a pupil at St Paul's School for Girls, where Holst was Director of Music.

I vow to thee, my country, all earthly things above,
Entire and whole and perfect, the service of my love:
The love that asks no question, the love that stands the test,
That lays upon the altar the dearest and the best;
The love that never falters, the love that pays the price,
The love that makes undaunted the final sacrifice.

And there's another country, I've heard of long ago,
Most dear to them that love her, most great to them that know;
We may not count her armies, we may not see her King;
Her fortress is a faithful heart, her pride is suffering;
And soul by soul and silently her shining bounds increase,
And her ways are ways of gentleness and all her paths are Peace.

22. *Immortal, invisible, God only wise*

A favourite of Her Majesty the Queen, and therefore often sung on royal occasions. It was written in 1867 by a minister of the Free Church, Walter Chalmers Smith (1824-1908), but its popularity is relatively recent. The tune, 'St Denio', is taken from a Welsh folk song.

Immortal, invisible, God only wise,
In light inaccessible hid from our eyes,
Most blessed, most glorious, the Ancient of Days,
Almighty, victorious, thy great name we praise.

Unresting, unhasting, and silent as light,
Nor wanting, nor wasting, thou rulest in might -
Thy justice like mountains high soaring above
Thy clouds which are fountains of goodness and love.

To all life thou givest, to both great and small;
In all life thou livest, the true life of all;
We blossom and flourish as leaves on the tree,
And wither and perish; but naught changeth thee.

Great Father of Glory, pure Father of Light,
Thine angels adore thee, all veiling their sight;
All laud we would render; O help us to see
'Tis only the splendour of light hideth thee.

23. *Jesus Christ is risen today*

The provenance of this resurrectional hymn is something of a mystery. An anonymous translation of an anonymous Latin hymn which can be dated back to a Munich monastery in the 14th century, it first appeared with its anonymous tune 'Lyra Davidica' or 'Easter Hymn', in a collection published in 1708. The translation has been substantially altered several times, and Charles Wesley added a redundant last verse for the Methodists.

Jesus Christ is risen today, Hallelujah!
Our triumphant holy day!
Who did once upon the cross
Suffer to redeem our loss:

Hymns of praise then let us sing, Hallelujah!
Unto Christ our heavenly king,
Who endured the Cross and grave,
Sinners to redeem and save.

But the pains that he endured, Hallelujah!
Our salvation have procured;
Now above the sky he's King.
Where the angels ever sing.

24. *Lead, kindly Light*

In 1833, the young theologian and Anglican vicar John Henry Newman (1801-90) was travelling in the Mediterranean when he was struck down by a fever that nearly killed him. 'My servant thought I was dying and begged for my last directions,' he recalled in his autobiography. 'I gave them as he wished, but I said, "I shall not die, for I have not sinned against light."'

Newman recovered slowly, but felt desperately homesick. On the way back to England, he took an orange boat from Palermo to Marseilles which was becalmed in the Straits of Bonifacio. Thus stranded, in an exhausted and emotional state, Newman was impelled to write this verse as a meditative poem called 'The Pillar of the Cloud', expressive of his longing for consoling Christian certainties in an age of mounting doubt. There has been much puzzlement over the nature of the 'kindly light' and the identity of the lost 'angel faces' in the last line. When challenged on these points, Newman replied crisply, 'I am not bound to remember my own meaning.'

He was displeased when the poem was turned into a hymn in 1845 – by which time he had converted to Catholicism, where congregational hymn-singing formed no part of divine service. To no avail: his words embodied the maudlin spirit of the age, to the point at which Queen Victoria asked it to be read to her as she lay dying. It was also the last hymn to be sung on the Titanic – not, as is sometimes said, as the liner was actually sinking, but at the final service given on board by the chaplain on the afternoon before the disaster.

Sung to several tunes, the one given here being 'Sandon', composed by Charles Purday.

Lead, kindly Light

Lead, kindly Light, amid the encircling gloom
Lead thou me on;
The night is dark, and I am far from home,
Lead thou me on.
Keep thou my feet; I do not ask to see
The distant scene; one step enough for me.

I was not for ever thus, nor prayed that thou
Shouldst lead me on;
I loved to choose and see my path; but now
Lead thou me on,
I loved the garish day, and, spite of fears,
Pride ruled my will: remember not past years.

So long thy power hath blessed me, sure it still
Will lead me on,
O'er moor and fen, o'er crag and torrent, till
The night is gone;
And with the morn those angel faces smile,
Which I have loved long since, and lost awhile.

25. *Lead us, heavenly Father*

Written in 1821 'for the children of the London Orphan Asylum' by a philanthropic architect James Edmeston (1791-1867), in whose office the far more distinguished Giles Gilbert Scott was apprenticed. Edmeston was the author of over two thousand such hymns, all directed at the poor and their neediness. J R Watson reminds us that this hymn is 'strikingly, even disturbingly, applicable to homeless children', its date of composition 'being a reminder that only fifteen years or so later Dickens was writing *Oliver Twist*.' Schoolboys have extracted some sniggering amusement at the application of the adjective 'dreary' to Jesus in the second verse, but it is intended in the sense of 'sorrowful' rather than 'boring'.

Sung to 'Mannheim', an old German chorale.

Lead us, heavenly Father, lead us

Lead us, heavenly Father, lead us
O'er the world's tempestuous sea;
Guard us, guide us, keep us, feed us,
For we have no help but thee;
Yet possessing every blessing,
If our God our Father be.

Saviour, breathe forgiveness o'er us:
All our weakness thou dost know;
Thou didst tread this earth before us,
Thou didst feel its keenest woe;
Lone and dreary, faint and weary,
Through the desert thou didst go.

Spirit of our God, descending,
Fill our hearts with heavenly joy,
Love with every passion blending,
Pleasure that can never cloy;
Thus provided, pardoned, guided,
Nothing can our peace destroy.

26. *Let all the world in ev'ry corner sing*

One of the few popular hymns written by a great poet, George Herbert (1593-1633). It appeared in his posthumous collection, *The Temple*, and was included in Wesley's seminal hymn book of 1737, though it went out of circulation in the 19th century. It owes a lot of its current popularity to the expansive tune 'Luckington', composed for a hymnal published in 1908 by the organist Basil Harwood. Lines three to six are intended to be sung antiphonally, between choir and congregation.

Let all the world in ev'ry corner sing
My God and King!
The heavens are not too high,
His praise may thither fly;
The earth is not too low,
His praises there may grow.
Let all the world in ev'ry corner sing
My God and King!

Let all the world in ev'ry corner sing,
My God and king!
The church with psalms must shout,
No door can keep them out;
But above all, the heart
Must bear the longest part.
Let all the world in ev'ry corner sing,
My God and King!

27. *Lord of all hopefulness*

Joyce Torrens (1901-1953), who wrote under the name of Jan Struther, became famous for a newspaper column in which she presented herself in the character of Mrs Miniver, a briskly sensible and humorous middle-class woman whose spirit seemed to embody a certain sort of plucky Englishness.

Mrs Miniver was turned into a film in 1942: heavily promoted in the USA, where it won the Oscar for Best Picture, it became crucial to the effort to woo American public opinion to support entry into the war against Hitler. There was not a single battle scene in the film, yet through its portrayal of the hardships suffered and overcome by a middle-class English family during the Blitz, it aroused the sympathy of ordinary Americans most effectively.

This hymn was written in 1929 at the request of Joyce Torrens' London neighbour, Canon Percy Dearmer of Westminster Abbey, for his new edition of *Songs of Praise*. Dearmer was delighted by its success, announcing in *Songs of Praise Discussed* (1933) that he was 'lately returned from a service of university students, who have speedily made it their favourite.'

J R Watson calls it 'entirely characteristic of its age, forward-looking, non-doctrinal, non-sectarian' and highlights its decision – quite daring at the time

– to replace 'thy' with 'you'.

Joyce Torrens herself – whose interest in Christianity was minimal – chose the shapely tune 'Slane', an old Irish melody.

Lord of all hopefulness, Lord of all joy

Lord of all hopefulness, Lord of all joy,
Whose trust, ever childlike, no cares could destroy,
Be there at our waking, and give us, we pray,
Your bliss in our hearts, Lord,
At the break of the day.

Lord of all eagerness, Lord of all faith,
Whose strong hands were skilled at the plane and the lathe,
Be there at our labours and give us, we pray,
Your strength in our hearts, Lord,
At the noon of the day.

Lord of all kindliness, Lord of all grace,
Your hands swift to welcome, your arms to embrace.
Be there at our homing, and give us, we pray,
Your love in our hearts, Lord,
At the eve of the day.

Lord of all gentleness, Lord of all calm,
Whose voice is contentment, whose presence is balm,
Be there at our sleeping, and give us, we pray,
Your peace in our hearts, Lord,
At the end of the day.

28. *Love divine, all loves excelling*

This is one of the loveliest hymns by Charles Wesley (1707-88), first published in 1747 in his brother John Wesley's collection, rather dauntingly entitled *Hymns for those that seek, and those that have, Redemption in the Blood of Jesus Christ*. But Charles Wesley must share some of the credit: he is thought to have been inspired, perhaps unconsciously, by a thoroughly pagan popular song of the day, 'Fairest isle, all isles excelling', written by John Dryden for Act 2 of Henry Purcell's opera *King Arthur* (1691), and the wonderful closing line turns out to be an unambiguous crib from a poem by Joseph Addison

When all thy mercies, o my God,
My rising soul surveys,
Transported with the view I'm lost
In wonder, love and praise.

Nobody has ever satisfactorily explained the meaning of 'changed from glory into glory' in the last verse, though it has been suggested that the line relates to 2 Corinthians 3:18: 'But we all, with open face beholding in a glass the glory of the Lord, are changed into the same image from glory to glory, even as by the Spirit of the Lord.'

Percy Dearmer points out 'how few of the earlier

hymns dwell upon the thought of God as Love. The popularity in recent years of this fine hymn of Wesley's is probably due to the fact that it does address God in this way.'

The tune 'Love Divine' is by John Stainer.

Love divine, all loves excelling

Love divine, all loves excelling
Joy of heav'n, to earth come down,
Fix in us thy humble dwelling,
All thy faithful mercies crown.

Jesu, thou art all compassion,
Pure unbounded love thou art
Visit us with thy salvation,
Enter every trembling heart.

Come, almighty to deliver,
Let us all thy life receive;
Suddenly return and never,
Never more thy temples leave.

Thee we would be always blessing,
Serve Thee as thy hosts above,
Pray, and praise thee, without ceasing,
Glory in thy perfect love.

Finish then thy new creation,
Pure and sinless let us be;
Let us see thy great salvation,
Perfectly restored in thee:

Changed from glory into glory,
Till in heav'n we take our place,
Till we cast our crowns before thee,
Lost in wonder, love and praise.

29. *Mine eyes have seen the glory*

People are often surprised that a woman wrote this fierily aggressive hymn, which has something of the broader national status in the US that 'Jerusalem' has in Britain. Its author Julia Ward Howe (1819-1910) was born of upper-class Unitarian stock. She married an abolitionist Bostonian doctor who worked with the insane and who had attempted to help the John Brown commemorated in the popular song 'John Brown's Body' – a deranged negro who in 1859 had killed five white men before setting up a kingdom of freed slaves in Virginia, only to be tracked down and hanged. (This account of the song's origins is disputed: some think it refers to another John Brown, who served in the 12th Massachusetts Regiment.)

In 1861, at the start of the Civil War, the Howes went out on to the Potomac river near Washington to watch a review of Unionist troops, where 'John Brown's Body' was lustily chanted. A friend who accompanied them suggested that some more uplifting words could be written to fit a tune that had obviously struck such a deep chord. The next morning, Mrs Ward Howe woke early and in a half-dreaming state – reflected in the almost hallucinogenic grandeur of the imagery, drawn on various biblical sources – scrawled out the verses. The poem was published on the front page of *The Atlantic Monthly* in February 1862 under the title

'The Battle Hymn of the Republic' and was soon widely reprinted with the 'John Brown's Body' tune, renamed 'Battle Song'. Mrs Ward Howe was paid only $4 for her efforts, but she had the not altogether happy reward of knowing that the words had helped the Unionist cause to its ultimate, blood-soaked victory.

Its influence has subsequently been manifold. It has long been the unofficial anthem of the American Republican party, and was also often cited in the speeches of Martin Luther King – his very last sermon quoted the hymn.

One survey believes that it has featured in over forty movies, the first being *Mother Machree* in 1928. At least two celebrated novels – John Steinbeck's *The Grapes of Wrath* and John Updike's *In the Beauty of the Lilies* – have borrowed from its lines for their titles.

It is a staple of the terraces and bleachers in both British and American football, its lyrics often adapted to fit a particular team (as in 'Glory, Glory, Man United'). Other adaptations include the first line of 'These things take time' by The Smiths. Outright parodies have been written by Mark Twain, Johnny Rebel and Garrison Keillor for *A Prairie Home Companion*.

Its currency extends to unlikely places around the world: in Turkey, it is a Boy Scout and Girl Guide song; in Japan, it has been used as an advertising jingle for Yodobashi cameras. It was played at the funerals of Winston Churchill, Robert F Kennedy and Ronald Reagan, and at the first 9/11 commemoration service on 14 September 2001.

Mine eyes have seen the glory

Mine eyes have seen the glory of the coming of the Lord;
He is trampling out the vintage where the grapes of
wrath are stored;
He hath loosed the fateful lightning of His terrible swift
sword:
His truth is marching on.

Refrain : *Glory! Glory! Hallelujah!*
Glory! Glory! Hallelujah!
Glory! Glory! Hallelujah!
Our God is marching on.

I have seen Him in the watchfires of a hundred circling camps;
They have builded Him an altar in the evening dews and damps;
I can read His righteous sentence in the dim and flaring lamps;
His day is marching on.

I have read a fiery gospel, writ in burnished rows of steel;
"As ye deal with my contemners, so with you my grace shall deal;"
Let the Hero born of woman crush the serpent with His heel;
Our God is marching on.

He has sounded forth the trumpet that shall never call retreat;
He is sifting out the hearts of men before His judgment seat;
O be swift my soul, to answer Him, be jubilant, my feet:
Our God is marching on.

In the beauty of the lilies Christ was born across the sea
With a glory in His bosom that transfigures you and me;
As He died to make men holy, let us die to make men free;
Our God is marching on.

He is coming like the glory of the morning on the wave,
He is wisdom to the mighty, He is succour to the brave;
So the world shall be His footstool, and the soul of wrong His slave:
Our God is marching on.

30. *My song is love unknown*

'But God forbid that I should glory, save in the cross of our Lord Jesus Christ, by whom the world is crucified unto me, and I unto the world.' This piece of Pauline mysticism, Galatians 6:14, is the root of an exquisite meditation by Samuel Crossman (1624-84), written in the style of George Herbert and published in 1664.

Dearmer primly states that it 'illustrates the fact that 17th-century Britain was free from the unwholesome treatment of the Passion which is shown, for instance, in the Spanish sculpture of that age', but its tone, as it both tells and reflects on the story of Christ's suffering, is almost painful in its emotional intimacy and humanity. Love is here 'unknown', because, as J R Watson suggests, it is 'unimaginable or because it is ignored, or simply because it is a love which is known to God but unknown to men'. Is there a more purely and hauntingly beautiful line in this book than 'Love to the loveless shown'?

The rhythmically supple tune 'Love unknown', which brought the hymn out of the obscurity into which the Victorians cast it, was composed in 1925 by John Ireland, who is said to have scribbled it down in fifteen minutes.

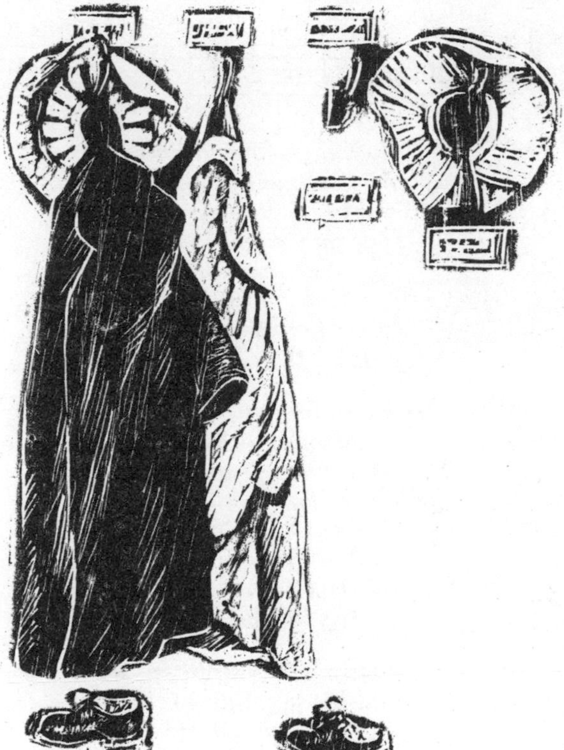

My song is love unknown,
My Saviour's love to me,
Love to the loveless shown,
That they might lovely be,
O, who am I,
That for my sake
My Lord should take
Frail flesh, and die?

He came from his blest throne,
Salvation to bestow;
But men made strange, and none
The longed-for Christ would know.
But O, my Friend,
My Friend indeed,
Who at my need
His life did spend!

Sometimes they strew his way,
And his sweet praises sing;
Resounding all the day
Hosannas to their King.
Then 'Crucify!'
Is all their breath,
And for his death
They thirst and cry.

Why, what hath my Lord done?
What makes this rage and spite?
He made the lame to run,
He gave the blind their sight.
Sweet injuries!
Yet they at these
Themselves displease,
And 'gainst him rise.

They rise, and needs will have
My dear Lord made away;
A murderer they save,
The Prince of Life they slay.
Yet cheerful he
To suffering goes,
That he his foes
From thence might free.

In life no house, no home,
My Lord on earth might have;
In death no friendly tomb,
But what a stranger gave.
What may I say?
Heav'n was his home;
But mine the tomb
Wherein he lay.

Here might I stay and sing,
No story so divine;
Never was love, dear King,
Never was grief like thine!
This is my Friend,
In whose sweet praise
I all my days
Could gladly spend.

31. Now thank we all our God

This majestic thanksgiving hymn was written by Martin Rinkart (1586-1649) during the Thirty Years War. Rinkart was the Lutheran pastor in a small town in Saxony, devastated by plague and then besieged by Swedes demanding an impossible 30,000 thaler as the price of withdrawal. After Rinkart's entreaties, the sum was reduced to 20,000 thaler, and Rinkart wrote the hymn to celebrate, taking the text from the apocryphal Ecclesiasticus 22:4. It was translated into English in 1858 by the splendid Catherine Winkworth, a German scholar based in Manchester, who was friendly with both Charlotte Bronte and Elizabeth Gaskell. The sturdy tune, 'Nun danket', was possibly composed by Rinkart himself.

Now thank we all our God
With hearts and hands and voices,
Who wondrous things hath done
In whom his world rejoices;
Who from our mother's arms
Hath blessed us on our way
With countless gifts of love,
And still is ours today

O may this bounteous God
Through all our life be near us,
With ever joyful hearts
And blessed peace to cheer us;
And keep us in his grace,
And guide us when perplexed,
And free us from all ills
In this world and the next

All praise and thanks to God
The Father now be given
The Son, and him who reigns
With them in highest heaven,
The one eternal God
Whom earth and heaven adore,
For thus it was, is now,
And shall be evermore.

32. *O come, O come, Emmanuel*

An Advent hymn, full of the Messianic prophecies of Isaiah, the origins of which in the Dark Ages remain obscure. It was translated from Latin into English by J M Neale(1818-66) in 1851, as 'Draw nigh, draw nigh Emmanuel' – a line he subsequently altered.

The tune, 'Veni Emmanuel' is not thought to be the genuine medieval plainsong melody it appears to be, but a clever pastiche – the musical equivalent of Victorian Gothic architecture.

O come, O come, Emmanuel,
And ransom captive Israel,
That mourns in lonely exile here,
Until the Son of God appear:

Refrain : *Rejoice! Rejoice, Emmanuel*
Shall come to thee, O Israel

O come, thou Rod of Jesse, free
Thine own from Satan's tyranny;
From depths of hell thy people save,
And give them vict'ry o'er the grave:

O come, thou Day-spring, come and cheer
Our spirits by thine advent here;
Disperse the gloomy clouds of night,
And death's dark shadows put to flight:

O come, thou Key of David, come,
And open wide our heav'nly home;
Make safe the way that leads on high,
And close the path to misery:

O come, O come, thou Lord of Might,
Who to thy tribes, on Sinai's height,
In ancient times didst give the law
In cloud, and majesty, and awe.

33. *O God, our help in ages past*

Sung on BBC radio minutes before the declaration of the Second World War, at Winston Churchill's funeral and so many Remembrance Day services, this hymn of solemn faith and imprecation is sometimes described as a second National Anthem. Percy Dearmer also suggested that it might be ranked as 'the greatest hymn in our language', though its austerity means that it has never been the most popular.

It is an adaptation by Isaac Watts (1674-1748), father of English hymnody, of the first verses of Psalm 90. He headed the text 'Man Frail, and God Eternal', and is thought to have written it in 1714, as Queen Anne lay dying and non-conformists like himself were deeply worried about a repeal of hard-won rights and liberties which a reactionary succession might bring. John Wesley included it in his 1739 hymnal, changing Watts' original first line 'Our God, our help in ages past' to its present form and omitting two weaker verses. It is this tweaked version which has been almost universally adopted ever since.

The tune, perhaps not equal to the grandeur of Watts' conception, is 'St Anne', by William Croft.

O God, our help in ages past

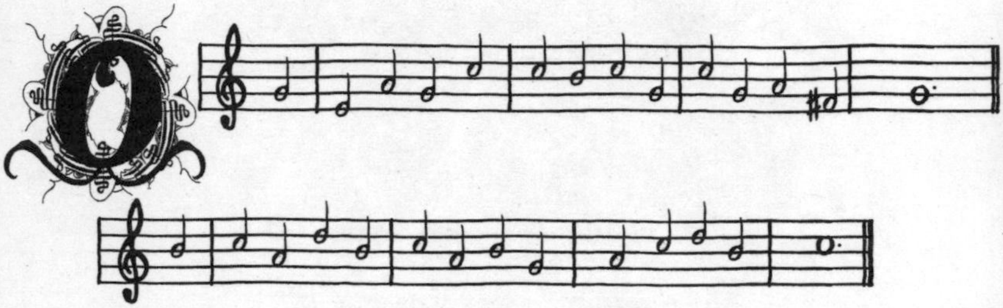

O God, our help in ages past,
Our hope for years to come,
Our shelter from the stormy blast,
And our eternal home.

Beneath the shadow of thy throne
Thy Saints have dwelt secure;
Sufficient is thine arm alone,
And our defence is sure.

Before the hills in order stood,
Or earth received her frame,
From everlasting thou art God,
To endless years the same.

A thousand ages in thy sight
Are like an evening gone;
Short as the watch that ends the night
Before the rising sun.

Time, like an ever-rolling stream,
Bears all its sons away;
They fly, forgotten as a dream
Dies at the opening day.

O God, our help in ages past,
Our hope for years to come,
Be thou our guard while troubles last,
And our eternal home.

34. O Jesus, I have promised

Bishops have been known to implore their clergy that this should not be sung at all the confirmations they attend,' lamented Percy Dearmer. But it was written specifically for such an occasion by the Revd. J E Bode (1816-74), who used it for his daughter and two sons. The opening of the last verse uses a similar idea to the last verse of 'Good King Wenceslas' – that of treading in a superior's footsteps.

The tune is 'Thornbury' by Basil Harwood.

O Jesus, I have promised
To serve thee to the end;
Be thou for ever near me,
My Master and my Friend;
I shall not fear the battle
If thou art by my side,
Nor wander from the pathway
If thou wilt be my Guide.

O let me feel thee near me:
The world is ever near;
I see the sights that dazzle,
The tempting sounds I hear;
My foes are ever near me,
Around me and within;
But Jesus, draw thou nearer,
And shield my soul from sin.

O let me hear thee speaking
In accents clear and still,
Above the storms of passion,
The murmurs of self-will;
O speak to reassure me,
To hasten or control;
O speak and make me listen,
Thou Guardian of my soul.

O let me see thy footmarks,
And in them plant mine own;
My hope to follow duly
Is in thy strength alone;
O guide me, call me, draw me,
Uphold me to the end;
And then in heaven receive me,
My Saviour and my Friend.

35. *O praise ye the Lord!*

A paraphrase of Psalms 148 and 150, written for the 1875 edition of *Hymns Ancient and Modern* by that book's driving organizational force, Sir Henry Williams Baker (1821-77), baronet and vicar of Monkland in Herefordshire.

The tune is 'Laudate Dominum' ; it can also be sung to "Hanover', which is the tune used for no. 36, overleaf.

O praise ye the Lord! Praise him in the height;
Rejoice in his word, ye angels of light;
Ye heavens adore him, by whom ye were made,
And worship before him, in brightness arrayed.

O praise ye the Lord! Praise him upon earth,
In tuneful accord, ye sons of new birth;
Praise him who hath brought you his grace from above,
Praise him who hath taught you to sing of his love.

O praise ye the Lord, all things that give sound;
Each jubilant chord re-echo around;
Loud organs, his glory forth tell in deep tone,
And, sweet harp, the story of what he hath done.

O praise ye the Lord! Thanksgiving and song
To him be outpoured all ages along;
For love in creation, for heaven restored,
For grace of salvation, O praise ye the Lord!

36. O worship the King, all glorious above

For 'sheer literary grace and beauty,' wrote Erik Routley, 'this may be one of the six finest hymns in the language. We all love it for its combination of effortless energy, high-spirited innocence, and the occasional touch of superb dignity.' Many others have agreed: 'beautiful in its Wordsworthian perception of an active, living universe,' claims J R Watson, 'it invests the vision of God with a chivalric grandeur.'

This undoubted masterpiece, inspired by Psalm 104, is the work of Sir Robert Grant (1779-1838), a barrister and MP who played a crucial role in a bill emancipating English Jews and who ended up as Governor of Bombay. The tune is 'Hanover' by William Croft.

O worship the King, all glorious above;
O gratefully sing his power and his love:
Our Shield and Defender, the Ancient of days,
Pavilioned in splendour, and girded with praise

O tell of his might, O sing of his grace,
Whose robe is the light, whose canopy space;
His chariots of wrath the deep thunder-clouds form,
And dark is his path on the wings of the storm.

The earth, with its store of wonders untold,
Almighty, thy power hath founded of old;
Hath 'stablished it fast by a changeless decree,
And round it hath cast, like a mantle, the sea.

Thy bountiful care what tongue can recite?
It breathes in the air, it shines in the light;
It streams from the hills, it descends to the plain,
And sweetly distils in the dew and the rain.

Frail children of dust, and feeble as frail,
In thee do we trust, nor find thee to fail;
Thy mercies how tender, how firm to the end,
Our Maker, Defender, Redeemer and Friend.

O measureless Might, ineffable Love,
While Angels delight to hymn thee above,
Thy humbler creation, though feeble their lays,
With true adoration shall sing to thy praise.

37. *Onward, Christian Soldiers*

This almost too famous expression of the Church Militant was penned in 1865 by the Revd. Sabine Baring-Gould (1834-1924). an outstanding example of the Victorian vicar who combined his pastoral work with antiquarian research. The son of an Indian cavalry officer, he was the author of several improving novels, significant folk-song collections and a 16-volume encyclopedia of the lives of the saints. Baring-Gould recalled that he knocked the verses off 'in about ten minutes' while he was in charge of a mission in Horbury Bridge, near Wakefield.

The hymn's original function was to accompany a Whit procession of Sunday School pupils through the local villages. On that occasion, it was sung to a tune adapted from the lugubrious slow movement of Haydn's Symphony in D, No. 53, 'L'Impériale', but today it is universally sung in the thunderously banal but irresistibly effective march composed in 1871 by Sir Arthur Sullivan. The melody is known as 'St Gertrude' in honour of Sullivan's friend Mrs Gertrude Clay-Seymer, whose house in Dorset Sullivan was staying in when inspiration struck. A later attempt by Gustav Holst to provide something more elegant was unsuccessful.

The hymn's huge popularity, especially in boys' schools, has recently been vitiated by anxiety about its unfashionably aggressive tone. Several politically correct hymnbooks exclude it altogether, and many sensitive clergy today do not permit it to be sung without mollifying alterations – 'Onward Christian pilgrims,/Working hard for peace' being one such revision. A gay version entitled 'Onward Christian homos' was composed for a LesBiGay service in Southwark Cathedral in 1996.

Powell and Pressburger's visionary wartime film *A Canterbury Tale* contains a moving scene in which a cinema organist turned soldier plays the hymn on the organ of Canterbury Cathedral at a service for a regiment about to leave to fight overseas.

Onward, Christian Soldiers

Onward, Christian Soldiers,
Marching as to war,
With the Cross of Jesus
Going on before.
Christ, the royal Master,
Leads against the foe;
Forward into battle,
See, his banners go!

Refrain : *Onward, Christian Soldiers,*
Marching as to war
With the Cross of Jesus
Going on before.

At the sign of triumph,
Satan's legions flee;
On then, Christian soldiers,
On to victory.
Hell's foundations quiver
At the shout of praise;
Brothers, lift your voices,
Loud your anthems raise.

Like a mighty army,
Moves the Church of God;
Brothers, we are treading
Where the Saints have trod;
We are not divided,
All one body we,
One in hope and doctrine,
One in charity.

Crowns and thrones may perish,
Kingdoms rise and wane,
But the Church of Jesus
Constant will remain:
Gates of hell can never
'Gainst that Church prevail
We have Christ's own promise
And that cannot fail.

Onward then, ye people,
Join our happy throng;
Blend with ours your voices
In the triumph-song;
'Glory, laud and honour
Unto Christ the King!'
This through countless ages
Men and angels sing.

38. *Praise, my soul, the King of heaven*

Of this jubilant hymn, Erik Routley wrote 'it finds a place in the repertoire of every Christian gathering, from royal weddings, to street corners … [it] is everything we want a hymn to be … it speaks clearly, but leaves room for the imagination. It has several arresting lines, yet the whole is homely enough for edifying of the simplest and the comfort of the most distracted.'

Its author is H F Lyte (1793-1847), who also wrote 'Abide with me'. It dates from 1834 and is based on Psalm 103. Its tune is 'Lauda Anima' by John Goss.

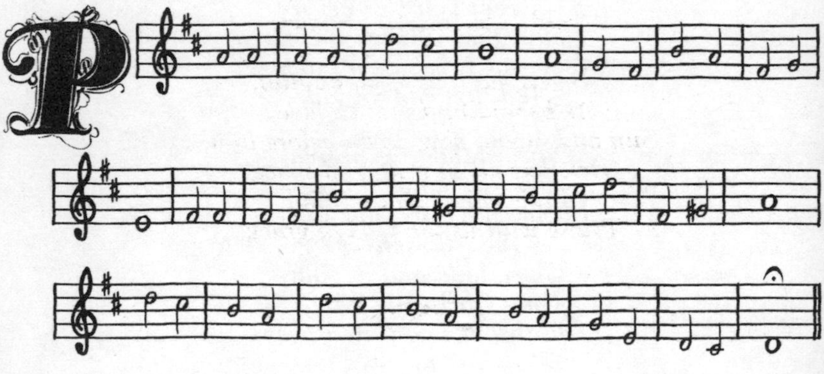

*Praise, my soul, the King of heaven,
To his feet thy tribute bring.
Ransomed, healed, restored, forgiven,
Who like me his praise should sing?
Praise him! Praise him!
Praise the everlasting king!*

*Praise him for his grace and favour
To our fathers in distress;
Praise him still the same for ever,
Slow to chide, and swift to bless.
Praise him! Praise him!
Glorious in his faithfulness.*

*Father-like, he tends and spares us;
Well our feeble frame he knows;
In his hands he gently bears us,
Rescues us from all our foes.
Praise him! Praise him!
Widely as his mercy flows.*

*Angels, help us to adore him;
Ye behold him face to face;
Sun and moon, bow down before him,
Dwellers all in time and space.
Praise him! Praise him!
Praise with us the God of grace!*

39. *Praise to the holiest in the height*

Like 'Firmly I believe and truly', this subtle encapsulation of the mysteries of God's providence and Christ's passion is an extract from the dramatic poem of 1865, *The Dream of Gerontius*, by John Henry Newman (1801-90). The editors of *Hymns Ancient and Modern* selected it from a thirty-five verse section entitled 'Hymn of the Angelicals'.

The fourth verse is omitted by stricter Protestants, since it suggests the alarmingly Catholic doctrine of transubstantiation. Ysenda Maxtone-Graham points out that the fifth verse offers an example of hymnal poetry in which the grammar and diction are so convoluted and compressed that the sense remains impenetrable.

The tune is by the Revd. Thomas Haweis, adapted by Samuel Webbe the younger in the early 19th century. The tune is 'Richmond', adapted from Thomas Haweis.

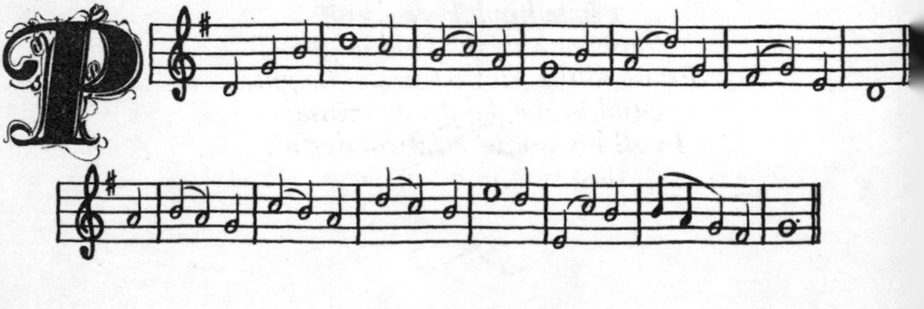

Praise to the Holiest in the height,
And in the depth be praise;
In all his words most wonderful,
Most sure in all his ways.

O loving wisdom of our God!
When all was sin and shame,
A second Adam to the fight
And to the rescue came.

O wisest love! that flesh and blood,
Which did in Adam fail,
Should strive afresh against the foe,
Should strive and should prevail;

And that a higher gift than grace
Should flesh and blood refine,
God's presence and his very self,
And essence all-divine.

O generous love! that he, who smote
In Man for man the foe,
The double agony in Man
For man should undergo;

And in the garden secretly,
And on the Cross on high,
Should teach his brethren, and inspire
To suffer and to die.

Praise to the Holiest in the height,
And in the depths be praise;
In all his words most wonderful,
Most sure in all his ways.

40. Ride on! Ride on in majesty!

Much revered by the Victorians but now almost forgotten, Dr Henry H Milman (1791-1868) was a prolific ecclesiastical historian, serving at either end of his career as Professor of Poetry at Oxford University and Dean of St Paul's Cathedral. Perhaps alone among hymn-writers he was also a successful playwright – his tragedy *Fazio* was a great hit at Covent Garden in 1818 and was subsequently translated into Italian.

This hymn for Palm Sunday was written in 1821. Its verse has been much admired, both for particular phrases (for instance, the oxymoron of 'lowly pomp') and for the way it creates a sense of foreboding – behind the jubilation it expresses at Christ's entry into Jerusalem is a sense of the ordeal that awaits him there and of God's larger purpose.

The tune is 'Winchester New', adapted from the chorale in the *Musikalisches Handbuch* (1690).

Ride on! Ride on in majesty!

Ride on! Ride on in majesty!
Hark, all the tribes hosanna cry;
Thine humble beast pursues his road
With palms and scattered garments strowed.

Ride on! Ride on in majesty!
In lowly pomp ride on to die:
O Christ, thy triumphs now begin
O'er captive death and conquered sin.

Ride on! Ride on in majesty!
The wingèd squadrons of the sky
Look down with sad and wondering eyes
To see the approaching sacrifice.

Ride on! Ride on in majesty!
Thy last and fiercest strife is nigh;
The Father, on his sapphire throne,
Expects his own anointed Son.

Ride on! Ride on in majesty!
In lowly pomp ride on to die;
Bow thy meek head to mortal pain
Then take, O God, thy power, and reign.

41. Rock of ages

A hymn 'strangely unlike any other', thought Percy Dearmer, and one that is certainly a muddle of images and excessively egocentric in its self-flagellation and abnegation – perhaps because it was the product of a slightly deranged mind. Augustus Montague Toplady (1740-78) was 'fanatical in a gross Calvinism, and most difficult to deal with'. He was minister of the French Reformed church in Soho, whence he engaged in aggressive pamphleteering and character-assassination (one of his victims, John Wesley, wisely decided that he was 'too dirty a writer for me to deal with'). Perhaps the tuberculosis which eventually killed him had something to do with it.

In 1776, he wrote a batty but oddly compelling article for *The Gospel Magazine*, in which he compared a rocketing National Debt, which could never be paid off, to the extent of human sinfulness. The mathematics of this would overwhelm even a quantum physicist (though apparently it omits to allow for leap years). We sin 'every second of our sublunary duration', he said, and 'our dreadful account stands as follows... At ten years old, each of us is chargeable with 315 millions and 36 thousand sins. At twenty, with 630 millions and 720 thousand' – ascending by degrees until at eighty, the grand total comes to '2,552 millions and 880 thousand.' But salvation is at hand: 'Christ hath redeemed us from the curse ... this, this will not only counter-balance but infinitely over-balance, ALL the sins of the WHOLE believing world.' At the conclusion, he published the hymn, with a heading 'A living and dying PRAYER for the HOLIEST BELIEVER in the world.'

There's an unsubstantiated tale that Toplady actually wrote the hymn on the back of a playing card when taking refuge during a storm in a cleft rock in a gorge in the Mendip Hills in Somerset – a plaque in Burrington Combe marks the spot. But there were many uses of the hymn's basic image in the Bible to inspire him, notably Numbers 20:11, where Moses smites a rock in the wilderness and water pours forth, various passages in Isaiah, and I Corinthians 10:4, where Paul speaks of believers who 'drank of that spiritual Rock that followed them: and that Rock was Christ.'

The American sage Oliver Wendell Holmes called 'Rock of Ages' the 'Protestant Dies irae', so thunderous was its rhetoric, and its stern moral tone appealed more to the Victorians than it does to us. Prince Albert is said to have murmured it deliriously on his deathbed; Gladstone not only translated the hymn into Latin and Greek but also commanded it for his funeral.

Any relation of the hymn to the song of the same name by the hard rock band Def Leppard – 'still rollin, rocknrollin' – is purely tangential.

The tune is 'Petra', by Richard Redhead.

Rock of ages

Rock of ages, cleft for me,
Let me hide myself in Thee;
Let the water and the blood,
From Thy riven side which flowed,
Be of sin the double cure:
Cleanse from me its guilt and power.

Not the labours of my hands
Can fulfil Thy law's demands;
Could my zeal no respite know,
Could my tears for ever flow,
All for sin could not atone:
Thou must save and, and Thou alone.

Nothing in my hand I bring,
Simply to Thy Cross I cling;
Naked, come to Thee for dress;
Helpless, look to Thee for grace;
Foul, I to the Fountain fly;
Wash me, Saviour, or I die.

While I draw this fleeting breath,
When my eye-strings break in death,
When I soar through tracts unknown,
See Thee on Thy judgment throne,
Rock of Ages, cleft for me,
Let me hide myself in Thee.

42. *Soldiers of Christ, arise*

Charles Wesley drew this hymn from Paul's letter to the Ephesians 6:11, 'Put on the whole armour of God, that ye may be able to stand against the wiles of the devil.'

'Paul was fond of military and athletic metaphors,' comments Erik Routley, but this hymn is an expression of collective force (like 'Onward, Christian soldiers') rather than individual struggle (like 'Who would true valour see'). Originally, Wesley warmed to his theme in 16 verses, but Victorian hymn-books mercifully cut the text down drastically. Percy Dearmer notes Wesley's 'sagacity in the use of imperfect rhymes' – for evidence of which read the second verse. The brightly optimistic tune is 'St Ethelwald', by William H Monk, written for *Hymns Ancient and Modern* in 1861.

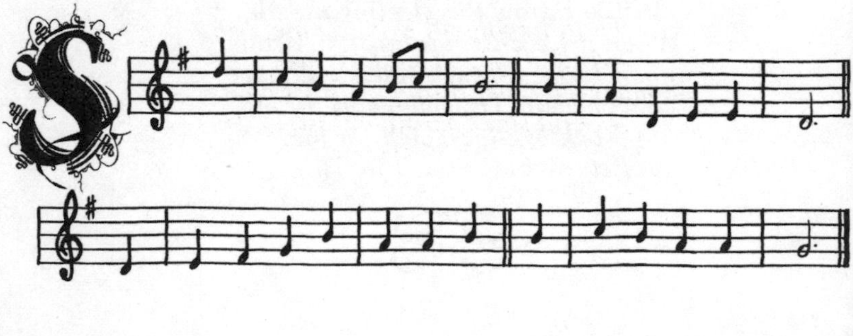

Soldiers of Christ, arise,
And put your armour on,
Strong in the strength which God supplies,
Through his eternal Son

Strong in the Lord of Hosts
And in his mighty power:
Who in his strength of Jesus trusts
Is more than conqueror.

Stand then in his great might,
With all his strength endued;
And take, to arm you for the fight,
The panoply of God.

From strength to strength go on,
Wrestle and fight and pray;
Tread all the powers of darkness down,
And win the well-fought day.

That, having all things done,
And all your conflicts past,
Ye may o'ercome, through Christ alone,
And stand entire at last.

43. *Stand up! Stand up for Jesus!*

A dreadful tale attaches to this American hymn. In 1858, shortly after preaching at a hugely successful mission in Philadelphia, the evangelist and abolitionist Dudley Atkins Tyng visited a barn on his farm.

Stretching out to pat a mule that was working a machine shelling corn, his sleeve caught in the cogs and tore his arm off. Hours later he was discovered, slowly bleeding to death. In his last moments, he whispered to one of his assistants, George Duffield (1818-88) – 'Tell them to stand up for Jesus.'

Duffield went sadly home and wrote the hymn as a tribute, which he read out as part of his next sermon. It was printed in a Sunday School newspaper and soon caught on, to the point that it was sung on both sides during the ensuing Civil War.

In England, it became a staple in public school services, and can be heard, slightly adapted as 'Stand up! – stand up for College', in Lindsay Anderson's great satire of those institutions, the film *If* … .

The tune is 'Morning Light', by G J Webb, originally composed for a parlour song, ''Tis dawn, the lark is singing', in 1837.

HYMNS

Stand up! Stand up for Jesus!

Stand up! Stand up for Jesus!
Ye soldiers of the Cross;
Lift high his royal banner,
It must not suffer loss.
From victory unto victory
His army he shall lead,
Till every foe is vanquished
And Christ is Lord indeed.

Stand up! Stand up for Jesus!
The trumpet call obey,
Forth to the mighty conflict
In this his glorious day.
Ye that are men now serve him
Against unnumbered foes:
Let courage rise with danger,
And strength to strength oppose.

Stand up! Stand up for Jesus!
Stand in his strength alone;
The arm of flesh will fail you
Ye dare not trust your own.
Put on the Gospel armour,
Each piece put on with prayer;
Where duty calls or danger
Be never wanting there!

Stand up! Stand up for Jesus!
The strife will not be long;
This day the noise of battle,
The next the victor's song.
To him that overcometh
A crown of life shall be;
He with the King of Glory
Shall reign eternally.

44. The Church's one foundation

Written in 1866 by Samuel Stone (1839-1900), as a conservative response to the controversy surrounding the 'liberal' Bishop Colenso of Natal, who had been threatened with deposition and excommunication after he published a book questioning the historical truth of the first five books of the Bible and the doctrine of eternal punishment.

The tune 'Aurelia' is by Samuel Wesley. When it was sung at the Lambeth Conference on 1888, it made the delegates 'feel weak at the knees, their legs trembled, and they really felt as though they were going to collapse.'

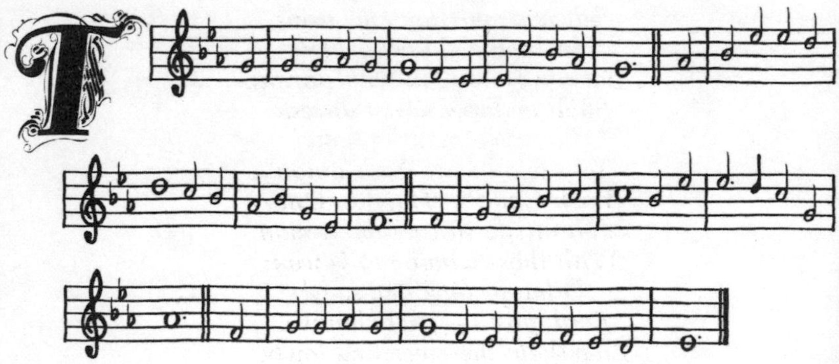

The Church's one foundation
Is Jesus Christ our Lord;
She is his new creation
By water and the word:
From heaven he came and sought her
To be his holy Bride,
With his own Blood he bought her,
And for her life he died.

Elect from every nation,
Yet one o'er all the earth,
Her charter of salvation
One Lord, one faith, one birth;
One holy name she blesses,
Partakes one holy food
And to one hope she presses
With every grace endued.

Mid toil and tribulation,
And tumult of her war,
She waits the consummation
Of peace for evermore;
Till with the vision glorious
Her longing eyes are blest,
And the great Church victorious
Shall be the Church at rest.

Yet she on earth hath union
With God the Three in One,
And mystic sweet communion
With those whose rest is won:
O happy ones and holy!
Lord, give us grace that we,
Like them the meek and lowly,
On high may dwell with thee.

45. The day thou gavest, Lord, is ended

A hymn which has often topped the charts in the BBC's *Songs of Praise* poll, much admired for its beautifully managed geographical progression and structure. It seems 'to draw into itself the beginning and end of things,' comments J R Watson. The work of a Cheshire vicar, John Ellerton (1826-93), who is said to have written it in 1870, as he made his nightly walk to teach at a Mechanics' Institute. He wrote much else subsequently, and according to Ian Bradley, 'while he lay in a state of semi-consciousness on his deathbed, hymns flowed almost unceasingly from his lips.'

Queen Victoria selected it as the hymn for her Diamond Jubilee in 1897, when it was sung in thousands of churches throughout her domains – 'As o'er each continent and island/The dawn leads on another day.' Even more poignantly, it was sung exactly a century later when Britain handed control of Hong Kong to China in 1997, closing a final chapter in the imperial story.

The waltzing tune, 'St Clement', is usually credited to the Revd. Clement Scholefield, commissioned by Arthur Sullivan for a collection of new hymn tunes. Ian Bradley plausibly argues that Scholefield's other compositions are so feeble that Sullivan might have acted as more than editor, pointing out that its 'highly sentimental streak and triple time signature' suggests the musical idiom of the Savoy Operettas.

Rick Wakeman's 1973 'concept' album, *The Six Wives of Henry VIII*, uses the tune as the theme for the 'Anne Boleyn' section.

The day thou gavest, Lord, is ended

The day thou gavest, Lord, is ended
The darkness falls at thy behest,
To thee our morning hymns ascended,
Thy praise shall sanctify our rest.

We thank thee that thy Church unsleeping,
While earth rolls onward into light,
Through all the world her watch is keeping,
And rests not now by day or night.

As o'er each continent and island
The dawn leads on another day,
The voice of prayer is never silent,
Nor dies the strain of praise away.

The sun that bids us rest is waking
Our brethren 'neath the western sky,
And hour by hour fresh lips are making
Thy wondrous doings heard on high.

So be it, Lord; thy throne shall never,
Like earth's proud empires, pass away;
Thy Kingdom stands, and grows for ever,
Till all thy creatures own thy sway.

46. *The King of love my shepherd is*

First printed in the Appendix to the 1868 edition of *Hymns Ancient and Modern*, this paraphrase of Psalm 23 was made by the collection's mastermind Sir Henry Williams Baker (1821-77). It was sung at the funeral of Diana Princess of Wales in 1997.

Only the third verse substantially differs from the biblical text, importing the popular Victorian theme of the Prodigal Son. It obviously remained close to his heart, because as his friend John Ellerton wrote, 'It may interest many to know that the third verse of this lovely hymn, perhaps the most beautiful of all the countless versions of Psalm 23, was the last audible sentence upon the dying lip of the lamented author.'

Ian Bradley finds this verse 'among the most honest and moving in all English hymnody... a wonderful evocation of both our erring human condition and the overflowing generosity of God's grace.' The tune 'Dominus regit me', by J B Dykes, dates from 1869.

The King of love my shepherd is,
Whose goodness faileth never;
I nothing lack if I am his
And he is mine for ever.

Where streams of living water flow
My ransomed soul he leadeth,
And where the verdant pastures grow
With food celestial feedeth.

Perverse and foolish oft I strayed,
But yet in love he sought me,
And on his shoulder gently laid,
And home rejoicing brought me.

In death's dark vale I fear no ill
With thee, dear Lord, beside me;
Thy rod and staff my comfort still,
Thy Cross before to guide me.

Thou spread'st a table in my sight;
Thy unction grace bestoweth;
And O what transport of delight
From thy pure chalice floweth!

And so through all the length of days
Thy goodness faileth never:
Good shepherd, may I sing thy praise
Within thy house for ever.

47. The Lord's my shepherd, I'll not want

Widely known by its tune 'Crimond', formerly ascribed to Jessie Irvine, daughter of the minister of the Scottish parish of that name, but now though to be the work of an Aberdonian tobacconist David Grant.

This paraphrase of Psalm 23 was first published in a Scottish psalter of 1650, but its indelible association with 'Crimond' is relatively recent, the result of broadcast performances by the Glasgow Orpheum Choir during the early days of the BBC and its selection for the wedding of Princess Elizabeth to Prince Philip in 1947.

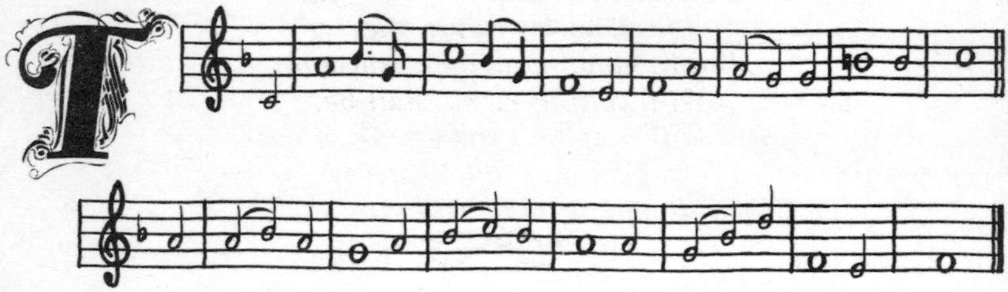

The Lord's my shepherd, I'll not want.
He makes me down to lie
In pastures green, he leadeth me
The quiet waters by.

My soul he doth restore again,
And me to walk doth make
Within the paths of righteousness,
E'en for his own name's sake.

Yea, though I walk in death's dark vale,
Yet will I fear none ill;
For thou art with me, and thy rod
And staff me comfort still.

My table thou hast furnishèd
In presence of my foes;
My head thou dost with oil anoint,
And my cup overflows.

Goodness and mercy all my life
Shall surely follow me;
And in God's house for evermore
My dwelling-place shall be.

48. *There is a green hill far away*

Written for Sunday school children in 1848 by Mrs C F Alexander (1818-95), author of 'All things bright and beautiful', as an Easter hymn expounding the doctrine of the Atonement in simple language. The 'green hill' is Mrs Alexander's fancy, without basis in the Bible, apparently inspired by a knoll that she used to pass on the road from her home in Derry which put her in mind of Calvary. 'Without' is a poetic locution, used to sustain the metre, for 'outside' – this has led to some confusion.

The tune is 'Horsley', by William Horsley, dating from 1844.

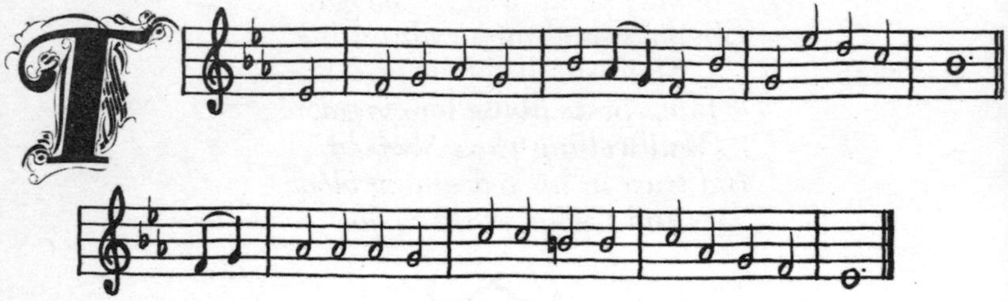

There is a green hill far away
Without a city wall,
Where the dear Lord was crucified,
Who died to save us all.

We may not know, we cannot tell,
What pains he had to bear,
But we believe it was for us
He hung and suffered there.

He died that we might be forgiven,
He died to make us good,
That we might go at last to heaven
Saved by his precious blood.

There was no other good enough
To pay the price of sin;
He only could unlock the gate
Of heaven, and let us in.

O dearly, dearly has he loved,
And we must love him too,
And trust in his redeeming blood,
And try his works to do.

49. *We plough the fields and scatter*

A German harvest festival hymn, originally written to form part of a play, by a Hanover-based scribbler Matthias Claudius (1740-1815), who published under the alias of 'Asmus'. Several of its verses were translated by a maiden lady living in Devon, Jane Montgomery Campbell, and published in 1861.

We plough the fields and scatter
The good seed on the land,
But it is fed and watered
By God's almighty hand;
He sends the snow in winter,
The warmth to swell the grain,
The breezes and the sunshine,
And soft refreshing rain.

Refrain : *All good gifts around us*
Are sent from heav'n above;
Then thank the Lord, O thank the Lord
For all his love.

He only is the maker
Of all things near and far,
He paints the wayside flower,
He lights the evening star.
The winds and waves obey him,
By him the birds are fed;
Much more to us, his children,
He gives our daily bread.

We thank thee then, O Father,
For all things bright and good;
The seed-time and the harvest,
Our life, our health, our food.
No gifts we have to offer
For all thy love imparts,
But that which thou desirest,
Our humble, thankful hearts.

50. When I survey the wondrous Cross

Another frequently nominated candidate for the laurel of the greatest hymn in the English language – Charles Wesley said he would give up all his own hymns to have written it, and George Eliot suggests its hold over ordinary folk when in her novel Adam Bede, she shows the Methodist preacher Dinah Morris reciting from it in her death throes. Vera Brittain, in her memoir *Testament of Experience* reports that it was Gandhi's favourite hymn, and it was sung at his memorial service in London in 1947.

It was written by Isaac Watts (1674-1748) and published in his volume *Hymns and Spiritual Songs* (1707). Although it draws on Paul's letter to the Galatians 6:14 ('God forbid that I should glory, save in the cross of our Lord Jesus Christ, by whom the world is crucified unto me and I to the world'), it is none the less extremely and intimately personal in its emotional involvement with the figure of the crucified Christ, dwelling on his pain and suffering with something of the intensity that one finds in baroque painting. This reflects the practice of contemplative praying proposed by Ignatius Loyola in his Spiritual Exercises and the Pietistic wing of the Lutheran church. Ian Bradley believes it to be the first hymn in English to use the personal pronoun.

The text has been much tinkered with: Watts himself changed the second line from 'Where the young prince of Glory dy'd', to avoid a false emphasis on 'the'. A fourth verse

His dying crimson, like a robe
Spreads o'er his body on the tree;
Then am I dead to all the globe,
And all the globe is dead to me.

has customarily been omitted since the Victorian era as being too graphic in its imagery of spent blood.

The tune 'Rockingham' was published in 1790, adapted from the earlier 'Tunbridge', by Aaron Williams. The latter has also been attributed, doubtfully, to C P E Bach.

When I survey the wondrous Cross

*When I survey the wondrous Cross
On which the Prince of glory died,
My richest gain I count but loss,
And pour contempt on all my pride.*

*Forbid it, Lord, that I should boast
Save in the death of Christ my God;
All the vain things that charm me most,
I sacrifice them to his blood.*

*See from his head, his hands, his feet,
Sorrow and love flow mingling down;
Did e'er such love and sorrow meet,
Or thorns compose so rich a crown?*

*Were the whole realm of nature mine,
That were an offering far too small;
Love so amazing, so divine,
Demands my soul, my life, my all.*

51. *Who would true valour see*

In the second part of John Bunyan's allegory *The Pilgrim's Progress* (1678-84), one of the figures encountered by Christian's wife and children as they follow his journey to the Celestial City in the company of Mr Great-Heart, is Mr Valiant-for-Truth. 'With his sword drawn and his face all bloody' after fighting off Inconsiderate, Pragmatick and Wildhead, he addresses them with this stirring poem, which has inspired generations of those going forth on the great adventures of life.

But it was only set to music a century or so ago. When Percy Dearmer and Ralph Vaughan Williams were preparing *The English Hymnal* (1906), they decided, as Dearmer put it, 'that some cheerful and manly hymns must be added to the usual repertory' and for that purpose adapted Bunyan's text, making alterations on the grounds that it wasn't originally conceived for congregational singing.

So 'Who would true valour see' became 'He who would valiant be', and out went the hobgoblins, lions and foul fiends, to be replaced with more dignified imagery – the first two lines of the third verse become the rather grey 'Since, Lord, thou dost defend/ Us with Thy Spirit'.

Churches today generally prefer Bunyan's more robust original, although the rousing traditional sea-song, known as 'Monks Gate', which Vaughan Williams transcribed from a Sussex source, has firmly established itself as the perfect musical accompaniment for both versions.

Who would true valour see

Who would true valour see,
Let him come hither;
One here will constant be,
Come wind, come weather;
There's no discouragement
Shall make him once relent
His first avowed intent
To be a pilgrim.

Who so beset him round
With dismal stories,
Do but themselves confound -
His strength the more is.
No lion can him fright;
He'll with a giant fight;
But he will have the right
To be a pilgrim,

Hobgoblin nor foul fiend
Can daunt his spirit;
He knows he at the end
Shall life inherit.
Then, fancies fly away!
He'll not fear what men say,
He'll labour night and day
To be a pilgrim.

52. *Ye holy angels bright*

Extracted and adapted in 1838 – by John Hampden Gurney (1802-62), Rector of St Mary's, Marylebone and 'a great meddler with other people's hymns' – from a 16-verse poem by a Presbyterian contemporary of Bunyan's, Richard Baxter (1615-91).

Imprisoned like Bunyan for his refusal to conform to the Anglican Settlement, Baxter was a cheerful soul who championed moderation and toleration. In the words of Marjorie Reeves and Jenyth Worsley: 'Unusually for a Puritan theologian, he found the road to heavenly contemplation through delight in natural beauty, in music and in the enjoyment of the senses generally.' Something of those qualities shines through this radiant hymn.

The tune, from 1770, is 'Darwall's 148th', originally used for Psalm 148, by John Darwall (1731-89).

Ye holy angels bright
Who wait at God's right hand,
Or through the realms of light
Fly at your Lord's command,
Assist our song,
For else the theme
Too high doth seem
For mortal tongue.

Ye blessèd souls at rest,
Who ran this earthly race,
And now, from sin released,
Behold the Saviour's face.
His praises sound,
As in his sight
With sweet delight
Ye do abound.

Ye saints, who toil below,
Adore your heavenly King,
And onward as ye go
Some joyful anthem sing;
Take what he gives,
And praise him still
Through good and ill,
Who ever lives.

My soul, bear thou thy part,
Triumph in God above,
And with a well-tuned heart
Sing thou the songs of love.
Let all thy days
Till life shall end,
What e'er he send,
Be filled with praise.

Carols

53. *Angels from the realms of glory*

Based on an old French carol, translated and adapted by James Montgomery (1771-1854), a radical journalist and publisher who first printed the verses in his own newspaper, the *Sheffield Iris*, in 1816. It is sung to 'Iris', a traditional French or Flemish tune.

Angels, from the realms of glory,
Wing your flight o'er all the earth,
Ye who sang creation's story,
Now proclaim Messiah's birth.

Refrain : *Gloria in excelsis deo!*

Shepherds in the field abiding,
Watching o'er your flocks by night,
God with man is now residing,
Yonder shines the infant Light.

Sages, leave your contemplations;
Brighter visions beam afar
Seek the great Desire of Nations;
Ye have seen his natal star.

Saints, before the altar bending,
Watching long in hope and fear,
Suddenly, the Lord, descending,
In his temple shall appear.

Though an infant now we view him
He shall fill his Father's throne,
Gather all the nations to him;
Every knee shall then bow down.

54. *Away in a manger*

An anonymous carol, transmitted via Lutheran émigrés to Pennsylvania, with a third verse written by John T McFarland (1851-1913). It first appeared in print in the US in 1885. A collection entitled *Dainty Songs for Little Lads and Lasses* mistakenly claimed it to have been 'composed by Martin Luther for his children and still sung by German mothers to their little ones'. The tune, 'Cradle Song' is by William James Kirkpatrick.

Nat King Cole, Linda Ronstadt and Sufjan Stevens are among those who have recorded memorable cover versions.

As Ian Bradley reminds us, many hymnals exclude this carol, perhaps because, of its unscriptural couplet, 'The cattle are lowing, the baby awakes/But little lord Jesus no crying he makes'. But its imagery remains a fundamental feature of childhood's Christmas.

Away in a manger, no crib for a bed,
The little lord Jesus laid down his sweet head.
The stars in the bright sky looked down where he lay,
The little lord Jesus asleep on the hay.

The cattle are lowing, the baby awakes,
But little lord Jesus no crying he makes.
I love thee, lord Jesus! Look down from the sky,
And stay by my bedside till morning is nigh.

Be near me, lord Jesus; I ask thee to stay
Close by me for ever and love me, I pray.
Bless all the dear children in thy tender care,
And fit us for heaven to live with thee there.

55. *God rest you merry, gentlemen*

The embodiment of the spirit of Victorian Christmas ever since it was sung to redeem Ebenezer Scrooge in Dickens' *A Christmas Carol*. The text was first published in 1833: both tune and words are anonymous, but they may have their origins among the 16th-century Waits bands that travelled round London singing in taverns. Some early printings of the carol change its sense slightly by putting the comma in the first line after 'you', but modern editors agree that this is incorrect.

It featured in Bing Crosby's 1945 *White Christmas* collection, which went on to become the best-selling Christmas record album of all time, and many other popular singers from Perry Como and Ella Fitzgerald to Mariah Carey have also covered it.

God rest you merry, gentlemen

God rest you merry, gentlemen,
Let nothing you dismay,
For Jesus Christ our Saviour
Was born upon this day:
To save us all from Satan's power
When we were gone astray.

Refrain : *O tidings of comfort and joy!*

In Bethlehem in Jewry
The blessèd babe was born,
And laid within a manger
Upon this blessed morn;
The which his mother Mary
Did nothing take in scorn.

From God our heavenly Father
A blessed angel came,
And unto certain shepherds
Brought tidings of the same,
How that in Bethlehem was born
The Son of God by name.

The shepherds at those tidings
Rejoicèd much in mind,
And left their flocks a-feeding
In tempest, storm and wind,
And went to Bethlehem straightway
This blessèd babe to find.

And when to Bethlehem they came,
Whereat this infant lay,
They found him in a manger
Where oxen feed on hay;
His mother Mary kneeling
Unto the Lord did pray.

Now to the Lord sing praises,
All you within this place,
And with true love and brotherhood
Each other now embrace;
This holy tide of Christmas
All anger should efface.

56. *Good Christian men, rejoice*

Freely translated and adapted by J M Neale (1818-66) from 'In dulci jubilo', a macaronic song (that is to say, one written in a mixture of languages – in this case, Latin and German) by the 14th-century Dominican monk Heinrich Seuse (or Suso), who claimed that it was inspired by some visiting angels who led him into a dance.

The melody is taken from a traditional German source, arranged in the late 19th century by John Stainer.

Good Christian men, rejoice
With heart and soul and voice!
Give ye heed to what we say:
Jesus Christ is born today;
Ox and ass before him bow,
And he is in the manger now.
Christ is born today.
Christ is born today.

Good Christian men, rejoice
With heart and soul and voice!
Now ye hear of endless bliss:
Jesus Christ was born for this;
He hath oped the heavenly door,
And man is blest for evermore.
Christ was born for this.
Christ was born for this.

Good Christian men, rejoice
With heart and soul and voice!
Now ye need not fear the grave:
Jesus Christ was born to save;
Calls you one and calls you all,
To gain his everlasting hall.
Christ was born to save.
Christ was born to save.

57. Good King Wenceslas

A carol for the Feast of St Stephen or Boxing Day, with no mention of the Nativity. Wenceslas was a tenth-century Catholic Duke of Bohemia also known as Vaclav the Good, and was martyred after being assassinated by his wicked brother, Boleslaw the Bad.

Wenceslas' remains are interred in St Vitus' cathedral in Prague, and he was recently made patron saint of the Czech Republic. His Saint's Day is September 28.

The verse is the invention of J M Neale (1818-66), and it was first published in 1853. The charitable giving which the carol promotes is as an old part of Boxing Day tradition (now, alas, supplanted by a spree at the first day of the sales). But nobody has ever understood why Neale makes Wenceslas feel impelled to take pine logs to a peasant who already lives next to a forest, nor is it clear what significance should be ascribed to the footprint in the snow mentioned in the last verse.

The tune selected by Neale, 'Tempus Adest Floridum' comes from a collection *Piae Cantiones*, published in 1582, where it is a spring hymn, clearly intended to accompany energetic dancing. Its roots are thought to be Scandinavian.

It was famously parodied by Spike Milligan in Goonish voices as 'Good King Ecclesias' and has been covered by musicians including Joan Baez and REM.

On The Beatles' first Christmas flexidisc, sent to their UK fan club members in 1963, the group performed several brief renditions of the carol, in a variety of arrangements, with John Lennon at one point singing a satirical set of lyrics, incorporating the names of several Hollywood stars.

Good King Wenceslas

Good King Wenceslas looked out
On the feast of Stephen,
When the snow lay round about
Deep and crisp and even;
Brightly shone the moon that night
Though the frost was cruel,
When a poor man came in sight,
Gath'ring winter fuel.

'Hither, page, and stand by me,
If thou know'st it, telling
Yonder peasant, who is he?
Where and what his dwelling?'
'Sire, he lives a good league hence,
Underneath the mountain,
Right against the forest fence,
By Saint Agnes' fountain.'

'Bring me flesh and bring me wine,
Bring me pine logs hither,
Thou and I will see him dine
When we bear them thither.'
Page and monarch forth they went,
Forth they went together,
Through the rude wind's wild lament
And the bitter weather.

'Sire, the night is darker now
And the wind blows stronger;
Fails my heart, I know not how,
I can go no longer.'
'Mark my footsteps, good my page,
Tread thou in them boldly:
Thou shalt find the winter's rage
Freeze thy blood less coldly.'

In his master's steps he trod,
Where the snow lay dinted;
Heat was in the very sod
Which the Saint had printed.
Therefore, Christian men, be sure
Wealth or rank possessing,
Ye who now will bless the poor
Shall yourselves find blessing.

58. *Hark, the herald angels sing*

Written by Charles Wesley (1707-88), and first published in 1739 as 'Hark, how all the welkin rings,/Glory to the King of Kings'. In 1753, for reasons that are not clear, the Wesleys' rival, the more Calvinistically inclined George Whitefield, altered the first two lines to their present form, as well as cutting a large number of extra verses. Ian Bradley regrets the excisions: Wesley's original proclaims what he calls 'an ecotheology', in which Christ is concerned 'with redeeming the whole environment and not just the human part of creation.' Various hymn-books, including the influential *English Hymnal* of 1906, have subsequently attempted to revive Wesley's original, without success.

The tune, 'Mendelssohn', was adapted in 1856 by W H Cummings (1831-1915) from the second movement of *Festgesang an die Künstler*, a choral cantata, composed in 1840 by Felix Mendelssohn (1809-47) and dedicated to marking the quatercentenary of Gutenberg's invention of movable type.

The carol is sung in the uplifting James Stewart movie *It's a Wonderful Life* and has more recently featured in an episode of the rather more disreputable cartoon series *South Park*.

Older readers may remember the parodic:

Hark! the herald angels sing
Beecham's pills are just the thing
Two for a woman, one for a child,
They will make you meek and mild.

Hark, the herald angels sing

Hark, the herald angels sing
'Glory to the new-born king,
Peace on earth, and mercy mild,
God and sinners reconciled.'
Joyful, all ye nations, rise,
Join the triumph of the skies;
With the angelic host proclaim,
'Christ is born in Bethlehem'.

Refrain : *Hark, the herald angels sing*
'Glory to the new-born king'.

Christ, by highest heaven adored,
Christ, the everlasting Lord,
Late in time behold him come,
Offspring of a virgin's womb.
Veil'd in flesh the Godhead see:
Hail, the incarnate Deity,
Pleased as man with man to dwell,
Jesus, our Emmanuel.

Hail, the heaven-born Prince of Peace:
Hail the Sun of Righteousness!
Light and life to all he brings,
Risen with healing in his wings.
Mild he lays his glory by,
Born that man no more may die
Born to raise the sons of earth,
Born to give them second birth.

59. *The holly and the ivy*

The symbolism of this anonymous carol relates to ancient fertility mythology and the association of the male with holly and good and the female with ivy and evil.

It may have accompanied some sort of ritual mating dance. Oddly, the ivy is never mentioned after the first line – are there some lost verses?

The text was first published in a broadside dated 1710, and may have originated somewhere in the Cotswolds. In 1861, it appeared in a collection of carols edited by one Joshua Sylvester, and the Victorians subsequently took it to heart.

The *New Oxford Book of Carols* points out that the refrain is 'incoherent and oddly irrelevant [standing] in the same aesthetic relationship to the verse as does Tower Bridge to the Tower of London, and is just the kind of Olde Englishe trumpery that a canny broadside publisher of 1710 might have strung together from stock to eke out his product.'

The tune, 'The Holly and the Ivy', was collected by Cecil Sharp who heard it sung by Mrs Mary Clayton of Chipping Campden in 1909. Other versions, by Allen Percival and Martin Shaw, have failed to supplant it.

Several other early carols pursue the holly and the ivy theme. One is found in a Tudor collection, set to a tune attributed to Henry VIII:

Green grow'th the holly
So doth the ivy;
Though winter blasts blow ne'er so high,
Green grow'th the holly.

The holly and the ivy

The holly and the ivy,
When they are both full grown,
Of all the trees that are in the wood,
The holly bears the crown.

Refrain : *O the rising of the sun*
And the running of the deer,
The playing of the merry organ,
Sweet singing in the choir.

The holly bears a blossom,
As white as any flower,
And Mary bore sweet Jesus Christ
To be our sweet Saviour.

The holly bears a berry,
As red as any blood,
And Mary bore sweet Jesus Christ
To do poor sinners good.

The holly bears a prickle,
As sharp as any thorn,
And Mary bore sweet Jesus Christ
On Christmas Day in the morn.

The holly bears a bark,
As bitter as any gall,
And Mary bore sweet Jesus Christ
For to redeem us all.

60. *In the bleak midwinter*

This exquisitely melancholy and evocative carol, imagining the Nativity in a snowy Northern landscape, was originally written by Christina Rossetti as a Christmas poem for an American magazine, *Scribner's Monthly*, in 1872. Ian Bradley wonders about its theology. 'Is it right to say that heaven cannot hold God, nor the earth sustain, and what about heaven and earth fleeing away when he comes to reign?' Yet few carols can express the quiet heart of Christmas more movingly.

It was set to music by Gustav Holst for the 1906 edition of *The English Hymnal* – the poignant and simple tune is known as 'Cranham'. Another equally lovely tune was composed by the organist Harold Darke in 1909, while he was a student at the Royal College of Music. It has the unusual distinction of varying the melody from verse to verse.

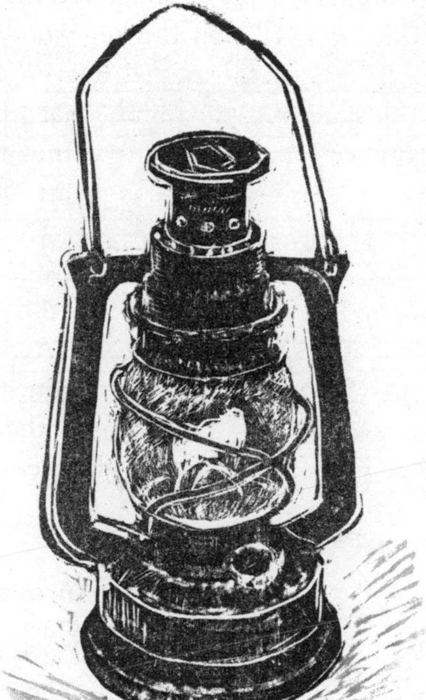

In the bleak midwinter

In the bleak midwinter
Frosty wind made moan,
Earth stood hard as iron,
Water like a stone:
Snow had fallen, snow on snow
Snow on snow,
In the bleak mid-winter,
Long ago.

Our God, heaven cannot hold him
Nor earth sustain;
Heaven and earth shall flee away
When he comes to reign:
In the bleak mid-winter
A stable-place sufficed
The Lord God Almighty
Jesus Christ.

Enough for him, whom cherubim
Worship night and day,
A breastful of milk,
And a mangerful of hay:
Enough for him, whom angels
Fall down before,
The ox and ass and camel
Which adore.

Angels and archangels
May have gathered there,
Cherubim and seraphim
Thronged the air -
But only his mother
In her maiden bliss
Worshipped the belovèd
With a kiss.

What can I give him,
Poor as I am?
If I were a shepherd
I would bring a lamb;
If I were a wise man
I would do my part;
Yet what I can, I give him -
Give my heart.

61. It came upon the midnight clear

An American carol, full of optimism about the future of the world, written in 1849 by Edmund Hamilton Sears (1810-76). a Unitarian minister descended from the Pilgrim Fathers, who served as pastor of a chapel in Wayland, Massachusetts. The traditional tune from Herefordshire, 'Noel', was arranged by Arthur Sullivan.

It came upon the midnight clear,
That glorious song of old,
From angels bending near the earth
To touch their harps of gold:
'Peace on the earth good-will to men,
From heaven's all gracious King!'
The world in solemn stillness lay
To hear the angels sing.

Still through the cloven skies they come,
With peaceful wings unfurled;
And still their heavenly music floats
O'er all the weary world:
Above its sad and lowly plains
They bend on hovering wing;
And ever o'er its Babel sounds
The blessed angels sing.

And ye, beneath life's crushing load,
Whose forms are bending low,
Who toil along the climbing way
With painful steps and slow,
Look now! For glad and golden hours
Come swiftly on the wing;
O rest beside the weary road,
And hear the angels sing.

For lo, the days are hastening on,
By prophet-bards foretold,
When, with the ever-circling years,
Comes round the Age of Gold;
When peace shall over all the earth
Its ancient splendours fling,
And the whole world give back the song
Which now the angels sing.

62. *O come all ye faithful*

The Latin version of this carol, 'Adeste Fideles', was written by John Francis Wade (1711-86), who fled England after the 1745 Jacobite rebellion to teach music in the school for British Roman Catholic exiles in Douai in France. It was first published in 1760, and it has been suggested that it might have incidentally served as a coded rallying cry for the Stewart cause. The English translation was made by Frederick Oakley and William Brooke in 1841.

The tune 'Adeste Fideles' is usually attributed to Samuel Webbe, and dated to 1782. But it is has also been ascribed to Wade himself or to the French composer Charles Favart. A mystery attaches to its Victorian reputation as 'the Portuguese hymn'. Some say that this came about because it was always sung at Christmas at the Portuguese Embassy, while others think that it was the work of King Joseph or King John of Portugal, or even the opera composer Marcas Portugal, also known as Portogallo.

The tune is often added nowadays to the lyric 'Why are we waiting?', performed spontaneously throughout the English-speaking world wherever queues form and delays frustrate.

O come all ye faithful

O come all ye faithful,
Joyful and triumphant,
O come ye, o come ye to Bethlehem;
Come and behold him
Born, the King of angels:

Refrain : *O come let us adore him*
Christ the Lord.

God of God,
Light of Light,
Lo, he abhors not the virgin's womb;
Very God,
Begotten not created:

Sing, choirs of angels,
Sing in exultation,
Sing, all ye citizens of heaven above:
Glory to God
In the highest:

Yea, Lord, we greet thee
Born this happy morning;
Jesu, to thee be glory given;
Word of the Father
Now in flesh appearing:

63. O little town of Bethlehem

On Christmas Eve in 1865 Phillips Brooks (1835-93), a gangling young American Episcopalian, rode the perilous journey from Jerusalem to Bethlehem, to assist at the midnight service in the Church of the Nativity. Two years later, back in Massachusetts, he was inspired by the experience to write this carol for his Sunday school. The Revd. Brooks – 6' 6" tall and capable of preaching at over 200 words a minute – was a favourite with children; when one woman told her daughter that he had died, the girl replied 'O how happy the angels will be.'

Brooks' carol was an instant success throughout the USA, but only came to England when Vaughan Williams introduced it in 1906, arranging it to the traditional tune 'Forest Green', which he had collected from peasants in Surrey in 1903.

O little town of Bethlehem,
How still we see thee lie!
Above thy deep and dreamless sleep
The silent stars go by;
Yet in thy dark streets shineth
The everlasting Light;
The hopes and fears of all the years
Are met in thee tonight,

O morning stars, together
Proclaim the holy birth,
And praises sing to God the king,
And peace to men on earth.
For Christ is born of Mary;
And, gathered all above,
While mortals sleep, the angels keep
Their watch of wondering love.

How silently, how silently,
The wondrous gift is given!
So God imparts to human hearts
The blessings of his heaven,
No ear may hear his coming;
But in this world of sin,
Where meek souls will receive him, still
The dear Christ enters in.

O holy child of Bethlehem,
Descend to us, we pray;
Cast out our sin, and enter in:
be born in us today.
We hear the Christmas angels
The great glad tidings tell:
O come to us, abide with us,
Our Lord Emmanuel.

64. *Once in royal David's city*

Written in 1848 by Mrs C F Alexander (1818-95, author of 'All things bright and beautiful' and 'There is a green hill'), with the aim of explaining to children the mystery of the Incarnation. The tune, 'Irby' dating from the following year, is by H J Gauntlett.

Famous for opening the annually broadcast Festival of Nine Lessons and Carols from King's College, Cambridge, where the first verse is always sung with heart-stopping purity by a lone treble.

Once in royal David's city,
Stood a lowly cattle shed,
Where a mother laid her baby
In a manger for his bed:
Mary was that mother mild,
Jesus Christ her little child.

He came down to earth from heaven
Who is God and Lord of all,
And his shelter was a stable,
And his cradle was a stall;
With the poor and mean and lowly
Lived on earth our Saviour holy.

And through all his wondrous childhood
He would honour and obey,
Love and watch the lowly maiden,
In whose gentle arms he lay:
Christian children all must be
Mild, obedient, good as he.

For he is our childhood's pattern,
Day by day, like us he grew,
He was little, weak and helpless,
Tears and smiles like us he knew:
And he feeleth for our sadness
And he shareth in our gladness.

And our eyes at last shall see him,
Through his own redeeming love,
For that child so dear and gentle
Is our Lord in heaven above;
And he leads his children on
To the place where he is gone.

Not in that poor lowly stable,
With the oxen standing by,
We shall see him: but in heaven,
Set at God's right hand on high;
Where like stars his children crowned
All in white shall wait around.

65. Silent night

A legend – much embroidered and variously related – surrounds this simple but universally loved Austrian carol. Here is one version of it.

On Christmas Eve in 1818, Joseph Mohr (1792-1848), the Catholic curate of Oberndorf, a Tyrolean village near Salzburg, was in despair. Mice had chewed away the mechanism of the church organ, and there was no way that it could be immediately repaired. Mohr's congregation needed something suitable to sing at midnight mass, so Mohr wrote these modest verses, inspired by a pastoral visit he had made early in the day to a mother and her sick baby.

Mohr – quite a rumbustious character, apparently, with a penchant for gambling, drinking and women - then ran round to his friend Franz Gruber, organist and headmaster in a neighbouring village, and asked him to write some gentle music for it. Gruber obliged with a gentle lullaby, and the carol was sung at midnight mass, Gruber accompanying on his guitar. After Christmas, the man who came to repair the organ was so impressed by Mohr and Gruber's little effort that he made a copy and passed it on to the Strasser Family – a precursor of the Von Trapps - who sang it at all their concerts and published it in 1838. A pretty tale, but probably largely fictional, not least because a manuscript of Gruber's tune suggests that it was actually written some two years before Mohr's lyrics.

What does it matter? 'Stille Nacht, heilige Nacht' has gone on to be translated into over 200 languages – it first reached English in 1858, thanks to a Miss Emily Elliott of Brighton, though the most commonly used version today was the work of an American bishop, John Freeman Young. It was sung by both sides at 25 December truces in the trenches of the First World War, and after Bing Crosby crooned it in the 1945 movie *The Bells of St Mary's*, it went on become as essential a feature of American Christmas rituals as the Yuletide Log and *The Nutcracker*.

A sixth slasher film in the series *Silent Night, Deadly Night* – 'You've made it through Halloween now try and survive Christmas' jeered the poster - is set for release in 2008.

Silent night, holy night

Silent night, holy night,
All is calm, all is bright,
Round yon Virgin Mother and Child,
Holy infant so tender and mild,
Sleep in heavenly peace,
Sleep in heavenly peace.

Silent night, holy night,
Shepherds quake at the sight,
Glories stream from heaven afar,
Heavenly hosts sing 'Alleluia!'
Christ the Saviour is born,
Christ the Saviour is born.

Silent night, holy night,
Son of God, love's pure light,
Radiant beams from thy holy face,
With the dawn of redeeming grace
Jesus, Lord at thy birth,
Jesus, Lord at thy birth.

66. The first Nowell

First published in a carol book in 1823, this anonymous text (to an equally anonymous tune, 'The first Nowell', arranged by John Stainer and generally felt to be horribly banal) is possibly of Cornish provenance – it features on an18th-century broadside sheet distributed in Helston.

There is no mention in St Matthew's gospel of shepherds seeing the star, so in the 1920s, Percy Dearmer changed the relevant words for his hymnal *Songs of Praise*, 'because children should not be taught mistakes of that kind'. But his pedantic emendation did not catch on.

The first Nowell

The first Nowell the angel did say
Was to certain poor shepherds in fields as they lay;
In fields where they lay, keeping their sheep,
On a cold winter's night that was so deep

Refrain : *Nowell, Born is the King of Israel.*

They lookèd up and saw a star,
Shining in the east beyond them far:
And to the earth it gave great light,
And so it continued both day and night.

And by the light of that same star
Three wise men came from country far
To seek a king was for their intent,
And to follow the star wheresoever it went.

This star drew nigh to the north-west;
O'er Bethlehem it took its rest,
And there it did both stop and stay
Right over the place where Jesus lay.

Then entered in those wise men three,
Full reverently upon their knee,
And offered there in his presence
Both gold and myrrh and frankincense.

Then let us all with one accord
Sing praises to our heavenly Lord,
That hath made heaven and earth of naught
And with his blood mankind hath bought.

67. *While shepherds watched their flocks by night*

Attributed to the sixth Poet Laureate Nahum Tate (1652-1715) and based on Luke 2: 8-14. It first appeared in print in 1702 and was arranged to 'Winchester Old,' an anonymous 16th-century tune, by William H Monk for *Hymns Ancient and Modern* (1861). Until 1782, it was the only Christmas carol officially sanctioned by the Church of England.

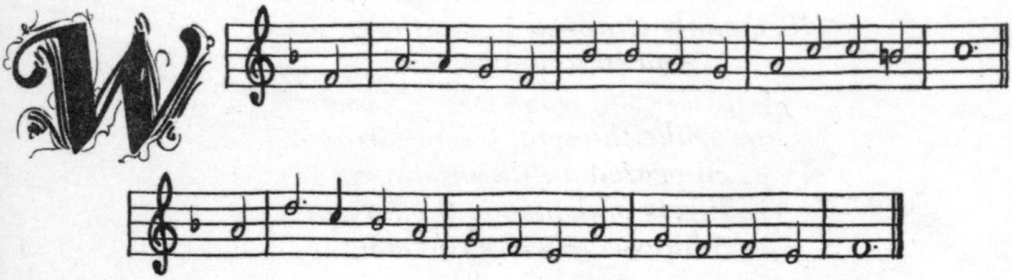

While shepherd watched their flocks by night,
All seated on the ground,
The angel of the Lord came down,
And glory shone around,

'Fear not' said he (for mighty dread
Had seized their troubled mind);
'Glad tidings of great joy I bring
To you and all mankind.'

'To you in David's town this day
Is born of David's line
A saviour, who is Christ the Lord;
And this shall be the sign:

The heavenly babe you there shall find
To human view displayed,
All meanly wrapped in swathing bands,
And in a manger laid.'

Thus spake the seraph and forthwith
Appeared a shining throng
Of angels praising God, who thus
Addressed their joyful song:

'All glory be to God on high
And to the earth be peace;
Good will henceforth from heaven to men
Begin and never cease.'

Miscellany

Wesley's Rules for the singing of hymns

1. Learn the tune
2. Sing them as they are printed.
3. Sing all.
4. Sing lustily and with a good courage
5. Sing modestly. Do not bawl.
6. Sing in time. Do not run before or stay behind.
7. Above all, sing spiritually. Have an eye to God in every word you sing. Aim at pleasing Him more than yourself, or any other creature. In order to do this, attend strictly to the sense of what you sing, and see that your heart is not carried away with the sound, but offered to God continually.

Hymns sung at royal weddings

PRINCESS ELIZABETH AND PRINCE PHILIP, 1947
Praise my soul, the King of heaven
The Lord's my shepherd

PRINCESS MARGARET AND ANTONY ARMSTRONG-JONES, 1960
Immortal, invisible, God only wise

PRINCESS ANNE AND MARK PHILLIPS, 1973
Glorious things of thee are spoken
The Lord's my shepherd
Immortal, invisible, God only wise

PRINCE CHARLES AND LADY DIANA SPENCER, 1981
Christ is made the sure Foundation
I vow to thee my country

PRINCE ANDREW AND SARAH FERGUSON, 1986
Praise to the Lord, the Almighty, the King of creation

Lead us, heavenly Father, lead us
Come down, o love divine

PRINCE CHARLES AND CAMILLA PARKER-BOWLES
Love divine, all loves excelling
Praise my soul, the King of heaven

Hymns sung at celebrity funerals

J F KENNEDY, 1963
Eternal Father, strong to save

WINSTON CHURCHILL, 1965
Battle Hymn of the Republic
Fight the good fight
Who would true valour see
O God, our help in ages past

JUDY GARLAND, 1969
Battle Hymn of the Republic

ELVIS PRESLEY, 1977
Heavenly Father
How great thou art

DIANA PRINCESS OF WALES, 1997
I vow to thee my country
Guide me, o thou great Redeemer

THE QUEEN MOTHER, 2002
Immortal, invisible, God only wise
Guide me, o thou great Redeemer

RONALD REAGAN, 2004
O love of God, how strong and true
Battle Hymn of the Republic
Amazing Grace
Sing with all the Saints

Hymns chosen by castaways on BBC's Desert Island Discs

JOHN BETJEMAN: Rock of ages
VALERIE HOBSON: Jerusalem
RICHARD DIMBLEBY: All people that on earth do dwell
LAURENS VAN DER POST: The first nowell (in Swahili)
FRANKIE HOWERD: Jerusalem
LEONARD CHESHIRE: Silent night
COLIN COWDREY: Praise my soul, the King of heaven
FIELD-MARSHAL MONTGOMERY: Battle Hymn of the Republic
ROY STRONG: For all the Saints
DUCHESS OF DEVONSHIRE: Holy, holy, holy
NOEL EDMONDS: Jerusalem
PRINCESS MARGARET: Guide me, o thou great Redeemer
WILLIAM WHITELAW: The Lord's my shepherd
LORD LICHFIELD: I vow to thee my country

Hymns which do not contain the words Lord, Jesus, God or Christ

I vow to thee my country
Lead, kindly Light
O worship the King, all glorious above
Rock of Ages
The spacious firmament on high
Who would true valour see

Hymns suitable for special occasions

CHRISTENING

Breathe on me, Breath of God
Come down, o love divine

Fight the good fight
Soldiers of Christ arise
Who would true valour see

GOING FORTH

Fight the good fight
Guide me, o thou great redeemer
I vow to thee my country
Lead, kindly Light
Stand up! Stand up for Jesus

COMING HOME

All people that on earth do dwell
Lord of all hopefulness, Lord of all joy
Praise to the holiest in the height

WEDDINGS

Love divine, all loves excelling
The King of love my shepherd is
The Lord's my shepherd

WAR AND PEACE

Battle Hymn of the Republic
Dear Lord and Father of mankind
Fight the good fight
Onward, Christian soldiers
Rock of Ages
Who would true valour see

Hymns written in the 20th century

I vow to thee my country
Lord of all hopefulness

A few of the thousand-odd singers who have recorded cover versions of 'Amazing Grace'

Christina Aguilera
Tori Amos
Michael Ball
Charlotte Church
Judy Collins
Placido Domingo
Bryan Ferry
Tennessee Ernie Ford
Aretha Franklin
Lesley Garrett
Mahalia Jackson
Janis Joplin
Kylie Minogue
Willie Nelson
Dolly Parton
Elvis Presley
Diana Ross
Rod Stewart
Hayley Westenra
The Blind Boys of Alabama
48th Highlanders Bagpipe Band
Mormon Tabernacle Choir
Toyota Pipes and Drums
Vienna Boys' Choir

Hymns chanted on the terraces

Abide with me (*FA Cup final*)
Battle Hymn of the Republic (*American football*)
Jerusalem (*The Ashes*)
Guide me, o thou great Redeemer (*Welsh rugby*)

Hymns sung in the last hours of the Titanic:

Eternal Father, Strong to Save
Lead, Kindly Light
Nearer my God to Thee
There is a Green Hill Far Away
O God Our Help in Ages Past

Parodies

Abide with me:
We've had no beer, we've had no beer today
(*First World War*)

All things bright and beautiful:
All things dull and ugly
(*Monty Python*)

God is working his purpose out
God is walking his porpoise out
(*prep schools*)

Mine eyes have seen the glory of the coming of the Lord:
Mine eyes have seen the orgy of the launching of the sword
(*Mark Twain*)

The Church's one foundation:
The Church's restoration
In 1883
Has left for contemplation
Not what there used to be
(*John Betjeman*)

We plough the fields and scatter:
We squirt the fields and scatter/
Our phosphates on the land
(*organic farmers*)

And did those feet in ancient time:
And did gay priests in ancient time
Work within England's church unseen?
And has the ministry of God
A lesbian calling always been?
(*action for gay and lesbian ordination*)

Bibliography

Ian Bradley, *Abide with me: The World of Victorian Hymns* (London, 1997)

The Daily Telegraph Book of Carols (London, 1996)

The Daily Telegraph Book of Hymns (London, 2005)

Percy Dearmer, *Songs of Praise Discussed* (Oxford, 1933)

S W Duffield, *English Hymns: Their Authors and History* (New York, 1886)

Hugh Keate and Andrew Parrott, *The New Oxford Book of Carols* (Oxford, 1992)

Marjorie Reeves and Jenyth Worsley, *Favourite Hymns: 200 years of Magnificat* (London, 2001)

Erik Routley, *Hymns and the Faith* (London, 1955)

The English Carol (Oxford, 1959)

Susan Tamke, *Make a Joyful Noise Unto the Lord* (Athens, Ohio, 1978)

Nicholas Temperley, *The Music of the English Parish Church* (Cambridge, 1979), vol. 1

J R Watson, *The English Hymn* (Oxford, 1997)

An Annotated Anthology of Hymns (Oxford, 2002)

Tyler Whittle, *Solid Joys and Lasting Treasure* (Bolton, 1985)

Website – www.cyberhymnal.com

Copyright/Permissions